World Wisdom
The Library of Perennial Philosophy

The Library of Perennial Philosophy is dedicated to the exposition of the timeless Truth underlying the diverse religions. This Truth, often referred to as the *Sophia Perennis*—or Perennial Wisdom—finds its expression in the revealed Scriptures as well as in the writings of the great sages and the artistic creations of the traditional worlds.

World Wheel IV-VII appears as one of our selections in the Writings of Frithjof Schuon series.

The Writings of Frithjof Schuon

The Writings of Frithjof Schuon form the foundation of our library because he is the preeminent exponent of the Perennial Philosophy. His work illuminates this perspective in both an essential and comprehensive manner like none other.

T0307008

World Wheel

Volumes IV–VII

Poems by

Frithjof Schuon

Foreword by
Annemarie Schimmel

Introduction by
William Stoddart

Translated from the German

World Wisdom

World Wheel
Volumes IV-VII
©2006 World Wisdom, Inc.

Library of Congress Cataloging-in-Publication Data

Schuon, Frithjof, 1907-1998.
  [Poems. English. Selections]
  World wheel, volumes IV-VII : poems / by Frithjof Schuon ;
foreword by Annemarie Schimmel ; introduction by William Stoddart.
      p. cm. -- (Writings of Frithjof Schuon series) (Library of perennial
philosophy)
  "Translated from the German."
  Includes bibliographical references and index.
  ISBN-13: 978-1-933316-31-4 (pbk. : alk. paper)
  ISBN-10: 1-933316-31-4 (pbk. : alk. paper) 1. Schuon, Frithjof,
1907-1998--Translations into English. 2. Religious poetry, German--
20th century. I. Schimmel, Annemarie. II. Stoddart, William. III. Title.
  PT2680.U474A2 2006c
  831'.914--dc22

                                                          2006030904

Cover: Frithjof Schuon
Photograph by Joseph E. Brown

Printed on acid-free paper in Canada

For information address World Wisdom, Inc.
P.O. Box 2682, Bloomington, Indiana 47402-2682

www.worldwisdom.com

Contents

Foreword

It seems that mystical experience almost inevitably leads to poetry. The great mystics all over the world used the language of poetry when trying to beckon to a mystery that lies beyond normal human experience, and the most glorious works in Eastern and Western religions are the hymns of the mystics, be they Sufis or Christians, Hindus or Zen monks. Different as their expressions are, one feels that the poetical word can more easily lead to the mystery that is hidden behind the veils of intellectual knowledge and which cannot be fettered in logical speech.

In the world of Islam, the love-intoxicated poems of Maulana Jalaladdin Rumi are considered by many to be "the Koran in the Persian tongue," and Rumi is only one of many intoxicated souls who expressed their love and longing, and their experience of the Divine Unity, in verse. And even those mystics who preferred a more "intellectual" approach to the Absolute couched their experiences in verse. The prime example is, of course, Ibn Arabi whose *Tarjuman al-ashwaq* translated his experience of the One, Unattainable Deity into the language of traditional Arabic poetry.

Taking this fact into consideration we are not surprised that Frithjof Schuon too felt compelled to write poetry—and, it is important to note, poetry in his German mother tongue. His verse sometimes reflects ideas and images of R. M. Rilke's *Stundenbuch*, in which the expert on mysticism can find some strange echoes of Ibn Arabi's ideas. This may be an accident, for mystical ideas are similar all over the world; but the German reader of Schuon's verses enjoys the familiar sound. This sound could not be maintained in the English translations of his poetry. Yet, as he himself explains, what really matters is the content, and here we listen to the thinker who, far from the intricate and complex scholarly sentences of his learned prose works, sings the simple prayers of the longing soul: God is the center, the primordial ground which comprehends everything, manifesting Himself through the colorful play of His creations. And it is the human heart which alone can reflect the incomprehensible Being, for humanity's central quality is divinely inspired love, which is the axis of our life.

I hope that Schuon's mystical verse will be read not only by English speaking readers but even more by those who understand German.[1] They will enjoy many of these tender lyrics which show the famous thinker in a very different light and from an unexpected side.

—Annemarie Schimmel, Professor Emeritus, Harvard University

[1] See Translator's Note on page *xvi*.

Introduction

Frithjof Schuon (1907-1998) was a sage, an artist, and a poet. During the last three years of his life, he wrote in German—his mother tongue—approximately 3,500 short poems, in 23 separate collections. In content, Schuon's German poems are similar to those in his English collection *Road to the Heart*, but they are much more numerous, and the imagery is even more rich and powerful. The poems cover every possible aspect of metaphysical doctrine, spiritual method, spiritual virtue, and the role and function of beauty. They express every conceivable subtlety of spiritual and moral counsel—and this not merely in general terms, but with uncanny intimacy, detail, and precision. They exhibit incredible sharpness, profundity, comprehensiveness, and compassion. They are his final gift to the world, his testament and his legacy.

Some of the poems are autobiographical, with reminiscences of places experienced: Basle and Paris, the fairy-tale streets of old German towns, Morocco and Andalusia, Turkey and Greece, the American West. Others evoke the genius of certain peoples, such as the Hindus, the Japanese, the Arabs, the Red Indians, and also the Cossacks and the Gypsies. Yet other poems elucidate the role of music, dance, and poetry itself. In one or two poems, the godless modern world comes in for biting, and sometimes fiercely humorous, comment:

> *Ein weltlich Fest: Lampenkristalle schimmern*
> *Im großen Saal —*
> *Und glänzende Gesellschaft, Damen, Herrn,*
> *Sitzen beim Mahl.*
> *Man spricht von allem und man spricht von nichts —*
> *Der Wein ist rot,*
> *Und so der Blumenschmuck.*
> *Doch keiner, keiner*
> *Denkt an den Tod.*

A worldly banquet: chandeliers glitter
In the large hall —
And brilliant society, ladies and gentlemen

Sit down for the meal.
They talk of everything and they talk of nothing —
The wine is red,
And so are the flowers.
But no one, no one
Thinks of death.

(*Stella Maris*, "The Celebration")

The poems embody both severity and compassion. They are powerfully interiorizing. Their content epitomizes Schuon's teaching, which he himself has summarized in the words Truth, Prayer, Virtue, and Beauty. For him, these are the four things needful; they are the very purpose of life, the only source of happiness, and the essential means of salvation. The poems convey these elements to the reader not only mentally, but also, as it were, existentially; their role is both doctrinal and sacramental.

The central role of prayer is powerfully expressed in the following poem entitled "*Panakeia*" ("panacea," the remedy for all ills):

Warum hat Gott die Sprache uns geschenkt?
Für das Gebet.
Weil Gottes Segen dem, der Ihm vertraut,
Ins Herze geht.

Ein Beten ist der allererste Schrei
in diesem Leben.
So ist der letzte Hauch ein Hoffnungswort —
Von Gott gegeben.

Was ist der Stoff, aus dem der Mensch gemacht,
Sein tiefstes Ich?
Es ist das Wort, das uns das Heil gewährt:
Herr, höre mich!

Why has God given us the gift of speech?
For prayer.
Because God's blessing enters the heart of him
Who trusts in God.

The very first cry in this life
Is a prayer.

And the last breath is a word of hope —
      Given by God.

What is the substance of which man is made,
      His deepest I?
It is the Word that grants us salvation:
      Lord, hear me!

                          (*Stella Maris*, "Panacea")

Many of the poems express the purpose of life with unmistakable clarity, for example:

Jedes Geschöpf ist da, um "Gott" zu sagen;
So musst auch du der Welt Berufung tragen,
O Mensch, der du der Erde König bist —
Weh dem, der seines Daseins Kern vergisst;

Dies tut nicht Tier noch Pflanze, ja kein Stein;
Dies tut der willensfreie Mensch allein
In seinem Wahn.
                Sprich "Gott" in deinem Wandern;
Es werde eine Gnade für die Andern.

Denn eine Aura strahlt vom Höchsten Namen —
Gebet ist Segen, ist der Gottheit Samen.

All creatures exist in order to say "God";
So must thou too accept the world's vocation,
O man, who art king of the earth —
Woe unto him who forgets the kernel of his existence;

No animal, no plant nor stone does this;
But only man, with his free will,
In his madness.
                Say "God" throughout thy life;
It will be a grace for others too.

For an aura radiates from the Supreme Name —
Prayer is blessing; it is the seed of the Divine.

                          (*Stella Maris*, "The Aura")

But the dread consequences of a wrong choice are not forgotten:

In Indien sagt man oft, dass Japa-Yoga
Stets Segen bringe — dass das Rāma-Mantra
Ein Wundermittel sei, das helfen müsse.
Dem ist nicht so, denn zürnen kann Shrī Rāma.

In India it is often said that *Japa-Yoga*
Always brings blessings — that the *Rāma-Mantra*
Is a miraculous means, that cannot but help.
This is not so, for Shrī Rāma can also show His wrath.

(Songs without Names I-XXXIII)

Und Gottes Zorn — er war zuvor schon da;
Denn Gottes Nein begleitet Gottes Ja.
Ihr fragt: war Gott zuerst nicht reine Milde?
Des Zornes Möglichkeit war auch im Bilde.

And God's anger — it was already there;
For God's No accompanies God's Yes.
You ask: is God not first and foremost Mercy?
The possibility of anger is also in the picture.

(Songs without Names II-LXXII)

Das Gottgedenken muss den Menschen ändern,
Denn zum Beleuchten gibt die Lampe Licht;
Wenn unsre Seele nicht verbessert wird,
Dann zählt das Sprechen frommer Formeln nicht.

Lass ab von falscher Größe — werde klein
Und selbstlos, und du wirst im Himmel sein.

God-remembrance must change man,
For the purpose of a lamp is to give light;
If our soul is not improved,
Then reciting pious formulas is of no avail.

Renounce false greatness — become small
And selfless, and thou wilt be in Heaven.

(Songs without Names IV-II)

Our human smallness is exposed without pity:

> *Lärmendes Nichts ist manche Menschenseel —*
> *Was bläht sie sich, als wär sie gottgeboren?*
> *Ein kurzer Erdentraum voll Eitelkeit,*
> *Ruhloses Tun — und alles ist verloren.*

> *Besinnet euch: seid klein, denn Gott ist groß.*
> *Er hat euch eine Heimat zubereitet*
> *Im Himmelreich: ein goldner Zufluchtsort —*
> *Wohl dem, der gegen seine Seele streitet!*

> Many a human soul is a noisy void —
> Why is she inflated as if born of God?
> A brief earthly dream, full of vanity,
> Restless activity — and all is lost.

> Remember: be small, for God is great.
> He has prepared for you a homeland
> In the Kingdom of Heaven, a golden shelter —
> Blessèd is he who fights against his soul!
>
> (*Adastra*, "Smallness")

Again and again, the poems return to the perplexing and agonizing problem of evil:

> *Da wo das Lichte erscheinet,*
>   *Da muss auch das Finstere drohen;*
> *Wundre und gräme dich nicht;*
>   *So will es das wirkende Sein.*
> *Siehe, die niederen Mächte*
>   *Bekämpfen heimtückisch die hohen;*
> *Da wo ein Abel erstrahlet,*
>   *Da ist auch ein finsterer Kain.*

> *Denn die Allmöglichkeit Gottes*
>   *Erfordert ja auch die Verneinung:*
> *Wahrheit und Friede sind himmlisch,*
>   *Irdisch sind Falschheit und Krieg.*
> *Ohne das Übel der Trennung,*
>   *Wo wäre das Gut der Verneinung?*

Ohne der Finsternis Treiben,
*   Wo wäre der Trost und der Sieg?*

Wherever light appears
    Darkness must also threaten;
Do not wonder and grieve,
    Existence will have it thus.
See how the lower powers
    Maliciously battle the higher;
Wherever Abel shines,
    There also is dark Cain.

For God's All-Possibility
    Also demands negation:
Truth and Peace are of Heaven,
    Earthly are falsehood and war.
Without the evil of separation,
    Where would be the good of reunion?
Without the work of darkness,
    Where would be solace and victory?

                                    (*Adastra*, "Cosmos")

No translation can possibly do full justice to the "poetry"—the meter, rhyme, verbal appositeness, allusions, music, inspiration—of the original German. Each German poem is a diamond—sparkling and clear, an architectural masterpiece full of light.

In his rich profusion of references to the many and varied cultural forms of Europe and beyond—the streets of the Latin Quarter, Andalusian nights, the Virgen del Pilar, the Macarena, sages such as Dante, Shankara, Pythagoras and Plato, the Psalms of David, Arab wisdom, the graces of the Bodhisattvas, Tibetan prayer-wheels, Samurai and Shinto, the songs of love and longing of many peoples—in all of these diverse cultures, Schuon captures the timeless message of truth and beauty which each contains, and renders it present in a most joyful way. When these cultural forms happen to be ones that the reader himself has known and loved, the joy that emanates from the poems is great indeed.

Schuon's long cycle of poems has already been compared to Rumi's *Mathnāwī*. I think that many of his poems can also be compared to the Psalms of David: they are an expression of nostalgia, of mankind's longing for, and ultimate satisfaction in, the Lord. Their main theme is trustful prayer to an ever-merciful God, and benevolence towards men of goodwill. First and foremost, the poems are instruments of instruction. As such, they are a powerful propulsion towards the inward.

A blessing lies not only in the quality of the poems, but also in the quantity—they constitute an all-inclusive totality. On the one hand, Schuon's German poems recapitulate the teachings contained in his philosophical works in French; on the other, they are an inexhaustible, and ever new, purifying fountain—a crystalline and living expression of the *Religio perennis*. They epitomize truth, beauty, and salvation.

—William Stoddart

Translator's Note

Schuon considered his poems didactic in nature and termed them "Sinngedichte," or teaching poems. With this in mind, the aim of the present English edition is to provide a literal rendering of the German text that remains as true as possible to the author's meaning. These translations are the work of William Stoddart, in collaboration with Catherine Schuon and Tamara Pollack. The translations draw extensively on Schuon's own informal, dictated translations. For a full appreciation of the lyrical resonance and musicality of the original, the reader is referred to the several German editions of these poems currently available.[1]

The last nineteen of these twenty-three collections are grouped under two primary headings, *Songs without Names I-XII* and *World Wheel I-VII*. The chronological order in which these collections were written, spanning three years from 1995-1998, is as follows: *Adastra, Stella Maris, Autumn Leaves, The Ring, Songs without Names I-V, World Wheel I, Songs without Names VI-XII,* and *World Wheel II-VII.*

---

[1] The complete German text of these poems is available in ten volumes from Editions Les Sept Flèches, 1062 Sottens, Suisse, www.sept-fleches.com, as a bilingual German/French edition. A complete bilingual German/Spanish edition is in preparation for 2007 from José J. de Olañeta, Editor, Palma de Mallorca, Spain. Selections can also be found in: *Liebe, Leben, Glück,* and *Sinn* (Freiburg im Breisgau: Verlag Herder, 1997); *Songs for a Spiritual Traveler* (Bloomington: World Wisdom, 2002); and *Adastra & Stella Maris: Poems by Frithjof Schuon* (Bloomington: World Wisdom, 2003).

World Wheel

Fourth Collection

I

God has been called a mighty fortress;
Blessèd is he who has found his way inside —
Who, behind God's wall, has recognized his true home,
The highest goods, and himself.

II

I think of God and let my cares depart —
Much idle thinking has only made them worse.
It is better I be not concerned with the world's deceit —
If only the good God be concerned with me.

III

"Blessèd be those who go
In and out of this house":
An inscription on a peasant's hut —
For the pious, God is always the center.

IV

My late grandfather used to say: "God brooks no mockery."
Whoever speaks in God's Name,
And prophesies evil things of his own accord,
Will regret it before the divine court of justice.

V

God and His Word will be with the one
Who clings to God. Whoever speaks from the Truth,
And not from the desires of his earthly soul,
Will be happy before the Face of God.

VI

Thou wilt not forever remain in trial;
Life's dark days will pass away;
Patience and hope will reach thee from Above.
In joy and sorrow thou wilt meet the Lord —
In all thy paths, let thy heart praise Him.

VII

Blessèd are those who seek not to know about this or that,
Because the Lord knows it;
Those who, when they see the essence of things,
Can resolve enigmas at God's behest.

VIII

Where Shrī Krishna dwells, *dharma*, virtue, shines;
Where dharma shines, there is *jaya*, victory —
When immortality awakens through God's grace —
Through the power of Light.

Where the Guru is, there wilt thou find
That which gives thee wings to overcome illusion.

IX

I read in a book that the best man
Is the one who considers himself the greatest of sinners —
This would mean a man who, fleeing from the world,
Out of sheer faith is no longer able to think.

An over-emphasis of sentiment works for some people —
Only sharpness of intelligence can lead to the truth.
Everyone seeks grace in his own way —
Love of truth is the highest path.

X

It is said that the ostrich in the desert
Quickly puts his head in the sand
If someone is pursuing him; whether true or not,
There is not merely foolishness in this story.

Because we too, we men — and rightly in this case? —
By not thinking, can avoid a needless struggle
With hostile surroundings. For it is better to feel nothing,
Than to lose one's head over the turmoil of the world.

XI

Ātmā and *Māyā* — this is the first discernment;
Then God and world, both of them being *Māyā*;
Then space and time: motionless space —
And time, which flows and dissolves like a dream.

XII

Matter, energy, form, and number,
Life, and consciousness — all of these
Within space and time. And above them
God's gaze — the luminous ray of the Spirit.

XIII

Body, soul, spirit. The body for this world,
The soul for the next. But the spirit,
The kernel of our being, has a special home —
Because it is divine, as it pleases God.

XIV

Always be with God and be not troubled —
Only the remembrance of God has weight.
Ask not about the Last Judgement —
The Face of God already shines today.

XV

A human being may love another human being —
Or a faithful animal, or a home with its dream;
What one has loved, and remains with us
In our earthly journey — one scarcely forgets.

Blessèd the man who, already early in life,
Does not forget where his heart's true home is.

XVI

The *yogī* says: appearances are nothing —
Only the Real should be real for us.
The man who sees not that God also dwells
In appearances, has no sense of God's presence.

XVII

One should not ask whether we shall find in Heaven
The things that we previously loved on earth —
One should understand, not what one wishes to think,
But what things say in themselves:
Namely that, in a noble image, is revealed
That which, in the Creator's realm, has never not been.

The Most High only gives more in Paradise;
Disappointment does not exist in God's meadow.

XVIII

Plato explained — and after him Augustine —
That everything good seeks to give itself;
The creative stream is infinite —
Yet what it brings is temporal, and will disappear.

But be not sad, for all that thou see'st
Stands written with God since the beginning —
So said Rumi. Not the wondrous work of beauty,
Only the earthly shadow-play disappears.

XIX

Think on God and be not troubled —
The world is like the sea agitated by the wind;
Thy little ship knows not what the waves want —
But in God's presence, thou art safe.

XX

It is no joy to write a poem in which one complains
About machines and technology,
And the evils of scientific hypertrophy —
For worse came, it was not long delayed —
Namely the two great wars, that bore
Witness to the cult of reason, which even today,
In spite of everything, one dare not attack.

XXI

I-ness is the enigma of enigmas —
God created man in the world as a witness:
We see that the meaning of earthly things
Is to bow before Him who created them —
That God, when He inscribed Being into nothingness,
Created the soul, that it might love Him and His works.

The I is unique in its essence,
Yet it becomes a countless host
Of uniquenesses. To overcome I-ness
Means to find one's true self in the One.

XXII

Melancholy and irascibility—may they be far from thee;
Do not let thyself be seduced by false impulses;
See how the evil spirits all too readily
Stir up war against the soul's peace.

The good spirits bring thee here below
That which is everything: Truth and Peace.

XXIII

It is important that the earnest seeker after truth
Should think correctly about various things —
And that none of the many vain prejudices
Distort the world and delude the mind.
Think not erroneously about things or peoples —
About what men are, and what they do.
Thou wilt not find the way to the Real
If faulty judgements constrict thy soul.

XXIV

On one night in the month of Ramadan,
The Koran came down to earth, it is said.
This night is celebrated every year,
Because what has been decided for all eternity —
And is written on the Guarded Tablet —
Allah can decree that it be revoked to-day.

For, in the face of predestination, God is free
To ordain that something else be written.

XXV

Remedies work, otherwise there would be
On earth no such thing as medicine.
The best physician is He who, in the Burning Bush,
Spake the great words: "I am that I am."

Say not that a remedy works by itself —
Be it strong or otherwise, God works therein.
The one cause encompasses the other —
In the deepest core, Almighty God, art Thou.

XXVI

Shaikh Ahmad was a holy Sufi Shaikh
Who led souls to the kingdom of the Most High;
People flocked to him — the sage gave everything
That liberates us from the curse of the Fall;
He made the soul like unto a lark —
O sweet magic of the God-filled sound.

XXVII

One sometimes forgets who one is —
The I becomes dispersed, and is no longer itself.
Be not caught up in the daily to-and-fro —
Thou wilt find thyself anew in the Divine;
In Him alone, and certainly nowhere else —
The alpha and omega are in the remembrance of God;
It will re-kindle thy love-song to God.

XXVIII

It is often said that one artist should not create
Like another; this is foolish enough —
It is natural that artists create the same thing,
When they drink from the same source.

It is not originality that is decisive,
But the value in itself, whoever the creator may be.
A Chinese vase has its own value —
But no one asks who was the potter.

Neither does one ask: who invented the style?
The goal is not individual glory — but the Truth.

XXIX

When I decorate a house or an apartment,
I keep in mind three artistic summits:
The Maghrib, Japan, and the South Seas. Simple and beautiful,
These are three formal languages, and three spiritual worlds.

For the ambience that is the framework
Of our everyday life is not indifferent;
It should not be dull or heavy,
But close to nature, simple and free.

The peasant's wooden house can also be a model;
A primordial dwelling — even in our time.

XXX

One must learn what is true and important;
However, this is not complete wisdom;
Thou wishest to know what is hidden and distant,
But thou needest something more — thou must learn how to think.

It is essential to think what is true —
But to think correctly is no less important.

XXXI

There was Tamerlane, and there was Alexander;
What one calls greatness is not always the same.
The great warrior who founds a world empire
Is not the wild man who destroys the world.

XXXII

What should one think of Napoleon?
His actions were a mockery of love of mankind.
The world was indignant at his fury;
But he died a believer — this suffices as consolation.
Was he nothing but a god of war?
His nature was not without good traits.

Faith is the greatest of all victories.

XXXIII

"There is no power or might, except with God"—
So it is said in the Koran. So let the battles rage;
They are bound by the stream of time —
The world's victory dance is soon scattered.

Is it not written on the walls of the Alhambra:
"There is no victor but God alone" —
Of human vainglory, nothing remains.

XXXIV

The *yogī* and the *yoginī* in *Ātmā*'s meadows
May love to be clothed with air alone;
Because, it is said, the aura of holy bodies
Wills to shine, in conformity with its *dharma*.

The good, Plato says, seeks to radiate —
The body wishes to paint Selfhood with light.

XXXV

God is for us the highest Other;
And within us, He is the deepest Self —
Thus highest "Thou" and deepest "I."
Both and neither is the Lord in Himself.

XXXVI

A spirit of contradiction dwells within our breast —
The evil one takes pleasure in obstructing and disturbing.
Hold fast to God, He will give thee the strength
To live according to the law of the straight path —
On which thou wouldst, and must, walk.

XXXVII

In our time, the ability to discern
Is minimal; one scarcely distinguishes
Between worth and worthlessness, between great and small —
Under the wilted tree, everything seems the same.
Lost is the Spirit's eagle-eye —
There are no longer criteria by which to judge.

XXXVIII

God gave me existence. What am I —
What is I-ness? A possibility
Of contemplating the world, of experiencing the Self —
Of loving God; and of beatitude

In a better world. We are made
For God, and for life beyond time.

XXXIX

"All is vanity," said Solomon.
Yes, and also no; certainly, and also perhaps;
The question is vain. The only important thing is
That thy soul reach the One Who created it.

XL

There are so many things that thinking cannot grasp.
Limitless space is unimaginable.
What does the brain comprehend?
It can scarcely grasp the primordial elements of existence.

The sage sees with the eye of his heart —
What one calls *Māyā*, perplexes him not.
What then is limitless, what is extension?
Through everything shines the Face of God.

So cease pondering, it leads to nothing —
See how the ray of the Most High breaks through the night.

XLI

What is the average man? Only late does he notice
That life's to-and-fro cannot go on forever;
That, after the succession of hours, days, and years,
The clock of life suddenly stands still —
That there is nothing more in the book to be read.
In reality, he has never been a human being.

XLII

Thou know'st thou canst not change the world —
Renounce it, let things be as they must be
In keeping with the laws of existence;
Becoming, disappearing. Ask not how and where.

Forget not thy Lord's Mercy —
A miracle, that liberates from destiny's might.
The essence of the web of this world
Is Being Itself: profundity and bliss.

XLIII

Lonely as thou mayst feel amongst men,
Yet thou hast thy God, and must not complain;
For He, who knows all thy paths,
Will help thee bear the solitude of the sage.

Certainly, thou art not separated from others —
Thou art alone only because thou art different.
Thou canst consort with others on the human plane;
They know not what thy solitude is.

XLIV

Certainly, what is foreign to truth is absurd —
But the fate of this illusion must be,
And it is not absurd; thou wilt not regret
The resignation to what must be.
Say "Yes," not to what thou shouldst not believe,
But to the possibility that was willed by God.

All-Possibility cannot give only the good —
The possible must also think of nothingness.

XLV

When melody resounds, the true is speaking;
When the true shines, God's melody
Resounds in it. The God-created All
Combines the light of truth with poetry.

It is the same with destiny: rigor calls for goodness,
And goodness calls for rigor, and so on and on.
Māyā plays its game with Yes and No —
Yet the last word belongs to Love.

XLVI

Where Thy Name is, there are Thy Truth and Presence.
There is nothing more in this world,
Nor will there be, from this day forth
Until the final Judgement.

XLVII

The soul belongs to the Lord, and not to the world;
The silence of the Spirit is the beauty of the True.
He who wants the happiness that is pleasing to the Lord,
Listens deep in his heart to the music of Truth.

Happy the man who does not find only half the Truth —
Who unites it with beauty of soul.

XLVIII

If thou encounterest ugliness of soul,
Forget it — let not poison enter thy heart.
Think of God, and be sure of this:
God abandons not the one who trusts in Him.

XLIX

What was the greatest moment in thy life?
And which event gave thee most happiness?
What was the high point on thy path?
On which "now" dost thou look back with joy?

It must have been the moment
God entered thy life's journey. The now — the time
That always is. For God is always there —
And so is thine Eternity, with Him, in Him.

L

Joy — joy given by God;
Good health and a long life.
But the Good in Itself is with the Supreme Lord—
So let thy life's star shine with Him.

Not every poem is the best of all—
But may this one too please my friends.

LI

East and West are the breasts
Of the mother of this world. See ye not
The sun's orbit — a circle in the vault of heaven?
This is its dance — God created the world from light.

Symbols build our universe —
Happy the man who, through the signs, contemplates the True.

LII

That one has the right — even the duty — to impart
A wise or beautiful word is obvious —
But silence may also convey it.
In God wisdom and beauty are related.

That which testifies to the Highest Good is beautiful;
In the beautiful, the spirit should see the True —
Happy the man who sees the one within the other.

LIII

Beyond-Being — a tremendous concept;
It is Reality, beyond Being and Existence,
Beyond the world of *Māyā* —
A greater Real does not exist.

LIV

In order to name to what lies beyond the *Māyā*-world,
Some have called Beyond-Being "Non-Being,"
And so doing, have turned the expression upside-down —
And not understood the possibilities of language.

LV

The German language lives on imagination,
And, with much feeling, expresses itself in images;
French is the language of concepts,
And thus the home of philosophers.
Le français définit; l'allemand veut peindre —
Dans l'Esprit les génies devraient se joindre;
For harmony is the spirit's bouquet of flowers.

The spirit looks out into the Infinite —
Le coeur qui tend vers Dieu, n'a rien à craindre.

LVI

Man is a door to Paradise —
But not everyone is man merely because he speaks.
To be man is a dignity: only he is human
Who has thrust aside evil —

The good, the wise, who has accomplished
His spiritual duty, and faithfully trusts in God.

LVII

Language is primordially human — because speech
Exists to break down the walls between us.
It is in the nature of language to be a point of view;
So choose between one soul and another.[1]

God spoke the first and best Word
While ye still lay in the sleep of non-existence.
In this Word lay the meaning of all wisdom —
God spoke, and thereby created the world: I AM.

LVIII

Serenitas — wise calmness of soul;
An undertone of noble longing
May also accompany it—for the soul feels
The breath of Paradise, though all too far away.

The soul is free, but under the spell of time —
Nevertheless: does not Eternity,
Heaven's radiance, touch thee? Thy heart may experience it,
When God so wills, in answer to thy striving.

LIX

Shankara-nature confers wise thinking;
Krishna-nature wants to bestow being and beauty —
And when both meet in one soul,
What comes from Heaven will blesses us doubly.

LX

The medicine man Yellowtail, my friend,
Could cure many incurable illnesses —
The good spirits came together
To hasten to the aid of the Red miracle-doctor.
"There are more things in heaven and earth
Than are dreamt of in your philosophy" —
Said Shakespeare.
                That which is not, can come to pass —
Do what God has taught you, and have strong faith.

LXI

Krishna-nature: the body of the *Avatāra*,
Whether man or woman, wondrously radiates a healing power;
As if it would bless the entire world with light —
As if it were the face of a Divinity.

Because Krishna, together with the *gopis'* dance,
Means that the sacred form leads to the Highest Good.

LXII

To accept what the Lord wishes to give us;
Not to take what He does not wish to give.
Not to love, what is unworthy of love to the Lord —
To love, what in God one ought to love.

LXIII

Vedānta, and with it *japa*, are for me
The quintessence of all religions;
Advaita and *nāma-japa* are the house
In which spirit and soul can dwell —
Perhaps within the framework of each religion;
The Throne of the One shines in all directions.

LXIV

"What dominates you is a vain striving for more,"
So says the Koran. If ye want more,
Then transcend yourselves; more is good
If it is the path that ye should desire —

The "more" in God. So always be ready
To understand deeply that ye are but little.

LXV

Love is there in order to love something,
Otherwise the world would sadden man.
One may ask why man loves woman —
Why? Because there is nothing else to love.

Because beauty breaks through all darkness —
One sees it, or one sees it not.

LXVI

There is much beauty in the world —
But much that one likes is vain.
And this is a hard nut to crack —
One cracks problems because one must.

Ephemerality, the illusory nature of things —
Only what bears witness to the eternal is justified.

LXVII

Life is a dream; contingencies —
Things that might be or might not be,
And yet had to be what they were;
Swinging between Reality and appearance —

Between the humdrum and the wondrous:
For God's nearness looks into thee.

LXVIII

Who says beauty, says woman —
Cosmology teaches us this, without where or how.
Who says woman, says weakness, wrote Shakespeare,
And he knew whereof he spoke.

Do not think that all this is unjust —
He who thinks otherwise knows mankind poorly.

LXIX

When you look at the world, do not see it as black —
Do not say that you miss perfection.
To be or not to be? What need does the world have to be,
When God alone is? So be silent — for He is.

LXX

Necessity — that which must be — is the axle;
Possibility is the wheel's rim.
The center is Being, which brings everything to pass;
The revolving circumference is Being's gift.

Thou art both, and neither. God alone is real —
But He lends to us from out of His Being.

LXXI

I no longer remember where or when I said
That Shakespeare's soul had no center —
That he burdened us, and also himself, with too much
Superficial and worldly chatter.
His plots he had no need to invent —
He found them in Italian stories.

This judgement was meant to be relative.
Everything that bears witness to greatness is a center —
Even within the realm of appearances.

Symbolism? If thou wishest to analyze a play,
Thou canst find it everywhere and always!

LXXII

The content of a woman's life is not only
Preoccupation with the little things of daily work —
Indeed she is great in what is small.
Her happiness is to be content with little —

And to give happiness to another.

LXXIII

First comes the beatitude of wise thinking,
And then the beatitude of holy being —
Everything is there. Say not of
What the Lord has given thee: it is mine.
Rather, look back towards the Giver —

Happiness of heart lies in forgetfulness of self.

LXXIV

What, in youth, was abstract —
Namely dying — in old age becomes concrete;
And what, in youth, was concrete,
Becomes abstract — the cup has been emptied.

LXXV

Whatever time may mean for thee, this alone counts:
That God fill thy soul with His nearness.
Ask not the sage where he should drink —
The Most High is here, and the cup is full.

LXXVI

Resignation in God and trust in God;
God-remembrance and contentment in His will;
Highest Truth and deepest Self —
Soul, be ready.

For, in earthly life there is nothing more
Than these doors — to eternity.

LXXVII

Without wisdom, life has no meaning,
And without beauty, we cannot live;
So let us strive to obtain the clear drink of Truth,
Together with the wine of Beauty.

For according to Plato: all harmony
Radiates from primordial philosophy.

LXXVIII

Folk-songs and lyrical poetry,
Songs of joy and sorrow — they lift us
Above the unrest and strains of everyday life;
A bouquet from the good days of yore.
The zither's nostalgia, the familiar melodies;
That is how it was — but now: all gone, all gone.

LXXIX

Space and time: stars great and small
Wander in time through the expanse of existence.
Space and time: in them are becoming and disappearing —
For this is the fate of all living beings;
But one day, when the Most High wills,
The coming and going also will cease.
Before God, even the largest worlds are small —
The final word belongs to Pure Being.

LXXX

I hold the outward world in honor,
But I pay it no heed when the inward calls me.
God created the universe, but, with wisdom and love,
He gave each thing its level.
And every earthly thing has its circle,
Its nature is known to the Most High alone.

LXXXI

What then is great and important in the earthly world?
I have said it often, but what is great, one gladly says again:
What counts is that one man invoke God's Supreme Name,
For himself alone, and without the world's knowing —
With God's Presence. The rest matters not.

LXXXII

Worldly greatness: someone did this and someone did that.
But what is man? This is what has been forgotten —
One saw only greatness of deeds, not smallness of being,
Not what we are. But one thing we know:
That we must pass away like the grass.

LXXXIII

Wisdom and poetry; woman, dance and music:
Truth and beauty in our earthly life;
But he who does not look back toward Him who gives it,
And does not see Him in everything, he lives in vain.

LXXXIV

Breathing and drinking — assimilating
What is airy and fluid; symbols of joy,
When the soul is illumined and renewed.

Light is the nourishment in the meadows of the Most High.

LXXXV

The reciprocity that unites us with God —
Happy the man who finds himself in the Creator.
God drinks the soul that drinks His Name —
God shines, while the soul's being is engulfed in light.

LXXXVI

Feeling happy through resignation to God's Will —
This the sage remembers;
From the very beginning, when, with God's blessing,
And with gratitude, he started on his path —
And likewise at the end of life's journey.
Blessèd is he who attains the goal of existence.

Our peace must be unconditional;
For God's Pure Being is absolute.

LXXXVII

Did not Jesus say: by every idle word
That you have spoken, ye shall be judged
On the Last Day? Then shall ye cry:
Would that the idle words had remained unsaid!

However: it may happen that the Lord
Shall erase what has been written, because another deed
Has much more weight on the Day of Judgement —
The good triumphs, and foolishness comes to naught.

God is without any fault, said Jesus;
So be ye perfect, even as the Lord is perfect.

LXXXVIII

It is strange how the ego weaves itself day by day —
How consciousness emerges out of nothingness;
If nothing were to happen, there would be neither I nor thou.

Blessèd is he, who lives above his egoity:
Who lives towards the True — yea, towards the deepest Self.

LXXXIX

Say yes to what is true because it is the truth —
Not because thou art a prisoner of wishful thinking;
Prejudice in favor of something and against everything
That contradicts it, to the point of persecution mania,
Is, as such, the work of the devil;
On the other hand, it can happen
That a mania shatters a false ideal;
Crusading mania, in an unscrupulous age,
Was compatible with sanctity —
An enigma before the Face of God.

XC

Insignifiant est ce qu'on exagère,
Say the French. What has been exaggerated
For emphasis, read it not;
What is alien to Truth is written in air.

XCI

"For verily after hardship cometh ease,"
It is said in the Koran; but no one knows
How and when this Word of God will reach him.

The soul would like to spread its wings,
Just as a lark, when morning dawns,
Feels like the light in heaven's vastness.

Our daily work has its earthly weight;
But if the soul looks toward the Most High,
All becomes easier — *cuando Dios quiere.*

And if patience is difficult for thee, complain not;
God helps the faithful servant to carry his burden.

XCII

Every man to his word. Keeping one's word is the virtue
Of the upright man who chooses faithfulness;
Self-domination is a yoga that
Ennobles the soul and strengthens the will.

Truth is from God. So be like unto It.
Blessèd the man who keeps his promise.

XCIII

When Asia was finally liberated from the West,
A weight was lifted from the hearts of many;
People said: this will be the golden age.

For prejudices make man dumb and blind;
The stubborn Guénonians did not know
That Asians too are only human.

Regarding Guénon's *East and West* — it would be nice
To see only the sacred in the East;
The sacred essence — not the emptiness of mere habit.

XCIV

A philosophical system is often like the desert sand —
Vain opinion is swirled around by the wind,
From an empty center to an empty rim —
Blessèd is he who remains silent when he has nothing to say.

XCV

It is astonishing how many living creatures,
Plants, animals, and men we know.
I call God not only a wise mathematician,
But also the richest of artists.
The world is woven not only of numbers —
It wishes to shine a thousandfold in beauty.

XCVI

The wind is a symbol in different ways:
It is the Spirit, that bloweth where it listeth —
From another point of view, it is an image of the nothingness
Of human stupidity, that swirls around in a circle.

Likewise stone is an image, either of heaviness,
Or of the unshakable Good;
Within man, it is the image of God-filled courage —
Happy the man who carries the eternal within him.

On the other hand, light is unambiguous —
Thou see'st in it but One thing, or thou see'st it not.

XCVII

Women's beauty is a quality conferred by Heaven —
But this gift should also be active
And encompass the whole soul,
So that the woman be what the Creator wished.

Outward charm flourishes for a few decades —
Blessèd is she who has made herself beautiful for the kingdom of Heaven.

XCVIII

There are many who do not find the strength
To overcome the flotsam of the past —
Things that should possibly be forgotten,
As one rolls up a silken scroll.

The Spirit confers on us an eternally youthful "now,"
Which replaces past illusion a thousand times —
May the True kindle our heart.

XCIX

In existence, everything is an up-and-down;
How could ye believe it to be otherwise?
Whatever happens, from the beginning to the grave —
Peace ye find in God alone.

The Lord made the world ambiguous —
At the same time, He brought us salvation,
And gave us His promise: ye are Mine.

C

Hold fast to God; and whatever thou needest in life
Will come from this basic law.
The Lord created the Spirit of Truth —
Blessèd is he who sees his path in the True.

True is what is willed by God — what is real;
Know thy Lord, and know what thou art.

CI

I have known women whose beauty in old age
Moved me deeply; they were untouched
By any trace of everyday grayness; only noble thinking
And noble sentiment shaped their features.

Happy the one who is not lax;
Hold faithfully to wise self-discipline.

CII

There is also holiness in children — see
How God finds a home in the heart of a child;
In a paradise of innocence — and before
Calculating reason has become hardened.

One also loves it when sages are childlike;
Did not Jesus say: become like little children.

CIII

It is curious how people admire a ruthless man
· Who kills people — nevertheless, what one loves
Is the hero who, despite his blood-stained sword,
Encourages nobility and patience.
If there were no warriors with a rough hand,
There would be no security in the land.

But what is useful is not always praiseworthy —
Therefore one speaks of a "two-edged sword":
Justice calls for violence and fire.

CIV

In many people there is a substance of soul
Which one would like to turn to good account —
That seems to be waiting for a higher, God-centered goal;
God grant that ye wait not in vain.
Thus every man is there for something good —
The question is whether he himself can see it.

CV

Who and what am I? Consciousness
Of the Highest Truth; and then the path to God;
The wise conclusion of the intellect —
There where the True is, there is Grace.
Cleave not to what thou art according to some dream —
Wish to be that which has a spiritual meaning.

CVI

That which awakens the presence of God,
The Supreme Name, is like a raiment
With which God covers His true Being.

Or it is deepest silence,
Extending from the heart to the Lord —
Existence keeps silent, only the One Will speaks.

CVII

Enlightenment often occurs in darkness —
Nel mezzo del cammin di nostra vita
Mi ritrovai per una selva oscura —
The night of the soul opens the path for thee.

Ma già volgeva il mio disio e'l velle
Sì come rota ch'igualmente è mossa —
L'amor che muove il sole e l'altre stelle.
In a dark forest ye seek a safe path —
The way of love leads to the sun and stars,
And after the trial comes the brightness of grace.

This is Alighieri's message:
Without the forest, ye cannot venture on the Path —
The ascension to the heavenly realm.

CVIII

Beauté oblige — this means, in other words:
If thou, O woman, art beautiful, thou must deserve it;
Beauty belongs not to thee — thou shouldst have
No such pretension in the face of God.

If God has lent thee such a grace,
Thou must draw from it the consequences —
In thy shape thy duty is apparent.

CIX

First: the Supreme Reality is *Ātmā*;
It has degrees — for *Māyā* is infinite.

Next: only one thing has meaning — God-remembrance;
Therefore it should guide all thy steps.

Thirdly: there is no better good here-below
Than God's presence — peace of heart.

Thou canst realize nothing without trust in God —
It helps thee face the future.

And then: the fact that He, the One, is unique
Means that He alone is the measure of things.

Finally: when worldly illusion has left thee,
What remains? There remains the One Self. —

The way to the Supreme Good is clear and straight.
There are six themes of meditation, but one sole path.

CX

Certitude of God, and with it, certitude of salvation —
The Lord is real; thou wishest to be of the blest.
God, and His own image — there is no better wisdom,
And no better activity, in this world.

CXI

If thou knowest thy Lord,
                    thou also knowest man;
If thou knowest man,
                    thou also knowest thy Lord.
Flee from what thy foolishness desires;
But what the Most High wishes, perform willingly.

Knowledge and will are the two poles
Unfolded in thee by God for thy well-being.
His Spirit and His Will are the star of existence.

CXII

In the desert sand near Mecca,
An unknown man, the leader of a caravan, went on his way
Beneath the vault of heaven. Some years later,
His empire dominated a third of the world.

Tiny cause, immense effect —
For in the son of the desert, God saw His instrument.
Blessèd is he who places himself in God's Will.

CXIII

Day by day, one lives through a dream —
Then, suddenly, the song comes to an end.
An end that is a beginning, according to God's Will —
In the eternal, all dreams come to a halt.

Blessèd is he who keeps the pact with God.

CXIV

Melancholy comes from the evil one, a proverb says —
And so do disturbing thoughts.
"A mighty fortress is our God."
If it please the enemy, he may himself waver.
Always take refuge in the Highest Good,
And leave the devil to rage in vain.

The one who seeks to disturb a pure soul,
Will sicken on his own poison.

CXV

A general once said: even the best rulers
Can scarcely govern an unruly people.
He who would and must rule, has no choice:
He wishes to sense a dignity in those he rules.
The ruler is the Lord's Hand on earth;
The people must be worthy of being well governed.
Whoever thinks that all his efforts are useless,
Will soon lose faith in himself.

CXVI

If thou hast cares, then say to thyself:
Nothing in life can remain the same;
Even things that are a burden on thy soul,
Are often a door to better days.

If thy heart reposes in God's nearness —
And if thou always thinkest of Him because this is the meaning of life —
Then thou knowest, despite all earthly burdens,
That all is well.

CXVII

Jesus — he had to be what he was;
He had God's Will as his companion.
Through his destiny, he was obliged to be the Christ —
According to a possibility willed by God.

All possibilities are in God's Hands —
And no power can turn them into something else.

CXVIII

Christianity is based on the manifestation
Of the Divinity: here there must be a Messiah,
Conceived as a drama, and intensely experienced —
The West needs the wine of such a faith.

Islam is based on the power of Truth:
Here the idea is everything: God is Pure Being;
Allah is One and Alone — praise be to God.
So bow down only before the Lord.

CXIX

The presence of God is the highest Word —
But if It wishes, It is deepest silence too.
God can show us His wondrous nearness
In both a yes and a no.

Whatever be the language of His nearness —
He gives Himself to us, and we belong to Him.

CXX

Auctoritas — the right to teach belongs
To the sage; and also to the man who speaks
Ex cathedra in the name of tradition.
The instrument of God receives the amen of Heaven.

Distinguish well between mere opinion
And that which, through the Spirit, is the presence of the Lord —
That which, beyond all doubt, is the seed of Pure Truth.

CXXI

One day follows another, and so do the nights —
We may wish that day and night would bring us something better;
May time overcome our anxiety,
And find us in better circumstances.

But patience! Look not at what happens to thee;
The Will of God is the end of the song.
Thou art not guilty of what fools do —
The wise man's affairs are in the Hands of God.

What thou art in God, no one can take from thee —
To thee belongs His presence; to fools, their schemes.

CXXII

Tanzīh, tashbīh — Arab concepts:
Incomparability and similitude;
Consciousness of Pure Divinity and symbolism —
A ray from the heavenly kingdom.

Out of these, spirit and soul are subtly woven —
But nothing is the equal of what God is in Himself.

CXXIII

Are not incomparability and similitude
Two rooms in the house of the same Truth?
Yes, because each testifies to the Highest Good;
And No, because the one excludes the other.

CXXIV

"Thou, Lord, art my shepherd;
                     and I shall not want;
In the dark valley, I will fear no evil.
Thou leadest me in green pastures —
Thy Word and Thy nearness comfort me."
Wherever I look is the light of Thy grace.

For what Thou willest is that I trust in Thee.

CXXV

Follow the path on which God guides thee;
If thou walkest with Him, He will walk with thee.
Happy the man who loses himself for the kingdom of Heaven —
If thou lookest towards God, He will look into thy heart.

Also: thou shouldst not grieve —
Thou art in God's Hands, and He will watch over thee.

CXXVI

Thou must not lose thyself in a world
In which souls freeze in the delusion of egoism.
Wherever the warm wind of goodness blows,
There is peace, and a happiness that never fades.

CXXVII

A friend of God said to himself: not this ego,
But Pure Being, confers happiness —
The divine and beatific Ipseity.

Such was Lallā: her garment was light and air;
Drunkenly, she danced back into her true Self.

CXXVIII

Neti, neti — "not this, not this" —
These are the first words of the Vedantic doctrine.
Only when the illusion of *Māyā* is dissolved
In thy spirit, canst thou honor Brahma.

Om, Shānti, Om — the quintessence of *Ātmā*'s song.
Where there is Truth, there is Peace.

CXXIX

Certitude of God, and with it, certitude of salvation:
On God's side, is the kingdom of the Supreme Truth;
On man's side, there is resignation to God's Will.
Peace be with you, and God's Presence at all times.

CXXX

Days and nights of Brahma — the waking and sleeping
Of the highest Reality. This is the world:
A being and a non-being; an immense dream
That flowers, and then falls into nothingness.

And so is man — a day and a night;
But in the deepest core of his heart
Is the One Who neither sleeps nor wakes.

CXXXI

A gigantic body in space, a grain of sand in the desert:
Even a speck of dust contains what that immense size offers.
And likewise: our spirit contains the All —
Even the Creator, who watches over the world.

CXXXII

God gives many consolations to man:
The first — divinely absolute — lies
In the Being of the Most High.

Yet our salvation is conditional:
Although the heart's power of faith suffices,
We still have to earn it.

Another consolation is the particular favor
That God gives to man according to his need.
We could also mention the little things
With which God, as if in play,
Rejoices the heart of the weary wanderer.

CXXXIII

The Name of God is the prayer of the heart —
As Bernard said: I love because I love.
Then comes petitionary prayer, and then thanksgiving —
Blessed the man who, timelessly, stands before the Most High.

CXXXIV

Truth in Itself — and with It, happiness in itself:
The one light comes from the other.
The miracles of the universe praise Thee —
O Truth, let me journey on Thy paths.

Where there is Reality, there is also blissfulness —
In this holy hour, and eternally.

World Wheel

Fifth Collection

I

Build on God and do thy duty —
Then thou wilt also find joy.
For what the Lord has given thee in thy spirit —
Thou must willingly proclaim.

Fundamentally, every heart is a messenger —
This lies in the nature of man. Whether ye know it
Or not, man's duty has this meaning:
That in everyone there is a message.

II

One day, I wanted to write nothing more;
The earth, I thought, revolves without me.
However: poems are not the author's work —
The poet keeps silent; the words write themselves.

III

Errare est humanum; in errore
Perseverare est diabolicum;
For lying minds that flee the truth,
What is crooked is straight, and what is straight is crooked.

Per animositatem; bitterness
In willful error comes from the devil.
It is much better to see one's own limits —
Self-doubt is better than obstinacy.

IV

Some say that the difference between good and evil,
Between beauty and ugliness, lies in arbitrary sentiment,
And not in the reality of outward things —
Good is only what is pleasing to man;

But one should know
That God made man a measure;
The human spirit bespeaks God's intention —
It watches over the nature of things.

Homo sapiens: if man could not distinguish
Between worth and worthlessness, between great and small,
There would be no measure; someone in the universe
Had to be the primordial measure of God.

V

Thou wishest that the beautiful would never fade —
Thus know: it is twice eternally young.
Firstly, because God gives beauty of age;
And then, because He loves the beautiful in its eternal essence.
The fountain of eternal youth is within you —
There is no withering in the heavenly realm within.

VI

God created the beautiful in the world
To be an image of His intention;
In the beautiful God reveals Himself —
So man must be true to his deepest heart.

Beauty is there to show God's essential intention —
And this man should understand.

VII

One would like life to stand still
When it makes us happy — but time moves on.
The world wheel turns whether thou wishest or not —
Blessèd is he who timelessly stands before the Most High.

VIII

Here, amidst the noise of things, man should know
That God Most High says "no" to what is idle —
So thou too must say "no" to outward things
That plague thee inwardly.
The wind blows — see, the dust has gone —
After all injustice, the "yes" of the Most High is victor.

IX

Truth and virtue; beauty and love;
If these alone remained to me,
The world could sink into the waters —
Let me drink only from the beautiful and true.

X

The wayfarer may be tolerably content
On his path — but he looks morose nonetheless;
For what he lacks, or seems to lack,
Is, in the storm, the protection of a mighty wall.

A man may be happy in his own way
Through his duty — but he knows the miseries
Of the world and the soul, and may seek help.

There is but one mighty fortress: prayer —
The faith that moves the mountain, the rock;

Blessèd the man whose heart lives from faith.

XI

Paranoia — the madman wishes to be the peak
Of a mountain; he cannot bear
To live as a man; for his happiness is only
To sit in judgement over others.

XII

Out of an evil something good must come —
Why? Because experience makes wise;
Because thou must overcome thy anger,
Not merely with thine own, but with God's strength —
This is self-evident. So be ready for the Lord —
Out of obedience serenity will shine.

XIII

Wisdom requires that we sometimes speak harshly;
The customer cannot drink, if he does not pay.
There is a good that falls from Heaven —
There is another — but for a high price.

XIV

If thou art with God, thou actually art
With everything that is lovable on earth.
But if thou art in the world, and only in it,
Thy heart is going in the wrong direction.

XV

Consoling warmth and pleasant coolness,
Along with the fragrance of roses and carnations —
These gifts give pleasure also in the heavenly realm;
Heat and cold exist only on earth:
Desert and ice are hardly celestial;
Yet, there is nothing that does not lead to God —
So do not complain about what adorns our earth.
For even in sand and snow, the power of Beauty works —
In them, God thinks of pure and empty Being.

XVI

I spoke of pure, but empty Being —
Being also is fullness, in a special sense.
It is not a quantity that one can measure,
It is a Unity, like sunshine —
The luminous, radiant garland of the love of God.

XVII

In Night and Ice — this is what Fridtjof Nansen called
His book on his journey to the farthest North;
Thus many journeys into the unknown
Have become symbols of a night that is hostile to life.
Let me praise what is near and solid —
North, South, East, West — home is the best.

However, what is remote can be the Center —
So turn toward the shrine of thy heart.

XVIII

Sir David Livingstone wanted to teach black people —
He wanted to convert them to the One good God.

Later he became an explorer in Africa —
He did too much, and could not be cured.

During his career, he struggled greatly —
He suffered from the world and from himself.

The heroic man's deep piety was clear —
His heart stood still as he knelt in prayer.

XIX

Firstly, thou must remain faithful to thyself;
In another respect, thou must progress and change.
A good disposition ought to bear fruit;
A bad one, thou must cast out of thy soul.
This is why thou art a wanderer on earth —
Let thine action sing the praise of the Most High.

XX

The human face is an open book:
Man should manifest intelligence and strength;
Beauty and goodness should radiate from woman —
May their souls bow down before the Truth.
Man, woman — the two are one human being;
God created them as His witness in the world.

XXI

In Islam, patience is always highly praised —
It is placed alongside Truth — *haqq* and *sabr*.
Where there is Truth, there is also peace —
There is no impatience in Heaven's meadows.

Patience — resignation to God's Will;
Doing — without haste or agitation — what we must do.

XXII

The cessation of mental agitation —
The peace that rises above the world;
This is the eternal, true Benares —
The Center that shows me my true self.

XXIII

Zen monks gaze on a white wall,
And concentrate on the absolute Void —
Beyond the web of world and reason,
So that no image, no sound, disturb *satori*.

Vacare Deo — neither mine nor thine —
It excludes everything, yet includes it all.

XXIV

God is the measure of our earthly works —
So let us do what has a meaning. But note:
What for the fool is of greatest importance,
Is the flight from his own nothingness.

XXV

The Christmas tree — a miracle from the forest,
On which candles shine and small globes hang;
It is no effort for a child's heart
To make of this an image of Paradise.

For us too, the little tree has meaning —
It evokes gratitude and innocence.

XXVI

Are our poems sometimes all too simple?
Perhaps, but the intelligent reader does not misunderstand them.

Among the readers there may well be children —
Whether big or small, we respect them no less.

Or perhaps mature elders read us —
The wise are not only among the old.

XXVII

If other things had happened to me, I would be another —
The fortuitous has woven me;
Certainly, what lay in me also had its effect —
And then: God raised me above myself.

XXVIII

The *individuum* is what cannot be divided —
God conceived man as an "I."
But there are souls that are split —
Thus many a one has brought himself to naught.

Do not confuse this with the two poles
That reveal an inner richness —
The soul that stands before its Creator,
Must keep for God what God has given it.

XXIX

The world of cities — Basel and Mülhausen were
The beginning. Then Lausanne for many years —
Gone, gone. Finally there came the wilderness —
The deep forest, that for me replaces everything.

XXX

Be Thou with me, and I will be with Thee —
God-remembrance is my sole concern.
Because the one whose heart pronounces not Thy Name —
His mind does not understand the meaning of existence.

XXXI

Thou art my God — I am in Thy hands;
I am on my path, where Thou hast willed.
And mayest Thou — Who knoweth me —
Always turn my steps towards Thee.

XXXII

In order to rejoice, one needs a reason;
But first of all comes the joy
That is unconditional, for it comes from Being —
And pure Being is there at all times.
Only what is from the Lord can gladden the heart.

Know that only in Being art thou real,
Before thinking that thine activity is thyself —
Before all this and that, be That which Is.

XXXIII

What we should do according to God's Word is simple;
Not simple is what we wish to do according to our own will.

Furthermore: "must" and "may"are not the same —
In God's Will alone is happiness here below.

XXXIV

There are different tendencies in the human breast.
Sentiment and passion animate the spirit of Jews and Arabs;
Everything is based
On faith and will.
India tends towards the pure Intellect —
Profoundly conscious
Of the eternal Real.
Reason alone remained for the West —
It yielded to outward appearances.
Something of each should be in every soul.

XXXV

Say but once: God — and a thousand vain deeds
Are extinguished, like candles in the wind;
Nothing can withstand the Absolute —
Behold how vanity disappears before the Word.

Follow the Truth within thyself —
See how the breath of the Most High kindles the heart.
Where God's Name resounds, there is victory —
The symbol that ends in the Almighty.

XXXVI

Firstly truth and virtue;
Then beauty and love.
Wisdom and its path; nobility and goodness —
All these manifest on earth the heavenly Nature.

XXXVII

The saying and the hearing of that
Which is unique seem to be nothing,
But they are everything. What they contain
And what they can bring thee, thou canst not measure.

XXXVIII

Many believe that we finally become gods
After thousands of cycles of existence.
Rather than entertain such an inflated illusion,
I prefer to be a God-willed man on earth —
Far be it that one should journey into a mythic naught.

XXXIX

I was called Frithjof; for my father dreamt
Of the wild fjords in the far north.
The soul feels at ease in Freyja's glow —
Frihet gar ut fron den ljungande Pol.

However: Basel is my home town —
Where the Rhine goes on its way,
Until it flows up into the North Sea;

Just as the soul finds its way to the Infinite.

XL

Invocation, and certitude of salvation,
                    are the elixir of life;
If there be any solace on earth,
                    hamin ast — then it is here.

Primordial prayer and God's blessing —
                    nothing better exists here below;
God's seed, which the earth
                    received into itself, brings Peace.

May the seed that falls to earth
                    blissfully become a flower.

XLI

Dieu soit béni — "Blessed be God" — but
In German, one would say: *Gott sei gepriesen* — "God be praised";
For there is no one who could bless God —
No one can have God's power of benediction.

Also: *béni soit son saint Nom;* this makes sense,
Because the Lord is more than His Name.

The language of the church often has expressions
That you must not follow absolutely —
One can praise God in every language.

XLII

"Physician, heal thyself" — many could heal themselves
If they did not have a secret pride in their veins;
And many souls would have been healed long ago,
Had they been capable to struggle with themselves.

XLIII

The evil one, it is said, can work miracles —
Still, Heaven has never pardoned him.
If he can do everything, yet one thing he cannot do:
This is to bow down before the Almighty.

XLIV

The pyramid stands on the edge of the desert,
In golden silence, in heat and sand.
I wanted to bow down inside it,
But I did not want to climb the outside —
I thought: the top is in the hands of the gods.

XLV

As Botticelli painted her, Venus emerged from the sea.
And so it is with the soul, when it emerges from the
Waters of knowledge. Bathing in the Spirit
Brings the victory of Truth.

A Hindu scripture says:
There is no lustral water better than knowledge.

XLVI

For the wise there is no "once upon a time" —
There is only the "now," which belongs to our Lord.
Leave fairy tales in the hands of children —
The Most High has taught us better things.

For wise souls, there is no time,
Said Meister Eckhart. Eternity is God's Kingdom,
Which never has not been.

Only timeless Pure Being can deliver us.

XLVII

The Most High will forgive thy foolish acts,
If thou knowest of thyself that they were foolish,
And if thou performest a pious act,
And thereby overcomest thy foolish delusion —
An act that God will judge with clemency.

For — whatever thy mistake may have been —
Self-knowledge, together with trust in God, is the best remedy.

XLVIII

In the far North: a walk in the night —
Almost terrifying is the vast sky
Which God created as a dome above us.

All around is the dark field of Mother Earth.
From above: a shining Presence —
The world of countless stars, close to God.

XLIX

Patience brings the soul much profit —
Yet impatience also has a meaning.
It is true that one kind of impatience is foolish,
When the soul cannot dominate itself;
But the other kind is logic:
It wills that everything follow a wise plan.
Thus things also happen with God
At the time that He conceives their being.

L

Think of God, then all is well.
Thou need'st not hesitate to do it;
He is the meaning of things, thy salvation —
And thy heart can repose in hope.

LI

May I not think of the many things
That are a consolation for me? Of course thou mayst do so,
But without forgetting the Most High —
So close thine eyes in faith.

On the Last Day — the Judgement of the Lord —
There is also a place for a wise equilibrium.

LII

Fanatics are people who think
That only exaggeration is praiseworthy;
An attitude that ends by twisting the True
Into a forced opposite.

Certainly, things are as they are —
God made them so with all rigor;
But on the other hand: in God's Pure Being,
Which penetrates everything, there is no narrowness.

LIII

Foolish curiosity has no limit;
But let us know what we must know.
We must not be angry with scholars
Because of that which constitutes their wisdom.

LIV

The Costa Brava — land of golden dreams;
Tossa and Cadaqués and Sant Feliú —
Bygone days. The coast of remembrance
Gives light and love. So close thine eyes.

LV

"It may be that the help of the Most High is near" —
So it is said in the Koran — much nearer than thou thinkest.
Thou may'st well ask: where is God's Might?
Thou knowest not — and suddenly it is there.

LVI

Sometimes a kind of sadness enters our soul —
There are indeed always reasons to grieve.
Happy are those who courageously stand at the Center,
Where other friends of God have stood before them —
Where God's Words of consolation do not fade away.

LVII

Kumbha-melā — a feast where naked sadhus
Sometimes fight, because holiness has
Different colors. Super-men?
No trace of them anywhere —

So it seems. But one man alone
May be there who brings a blessing.

LVIII

Lallā had two reasons for going naked
Before the people: an inner one,
Because, in her heart, she had found the Self;
And an outer one, because the goddess freely shines
Through all feminine beauty,
In order to manifest Heaven to the whole world.

LIX

We need two things: consolation and help;
Consolation, so that our soul does not grieve;
Help, so that we know what to do —
So that doubt does not paralyze our action;
So that God may accomplish what we ourselves cannot do —
So that, filled with trust, we may be at peace;
In pure love, and in the knowledge of God.

LX

Being and Self: act and contemplation;
The highest Outward and the deepest Inward.

Happy the one who drinks from the well-spring of Primordial Being —
And who is penetrated by the primordial song of the Self.

LXI

The essential is that I strive towards my goal,
And that I shun everything that resists it;
Only vexation comes when I move in darkness;
If I think of God, I am in joy,
And know why I am — and why I live.

LXII

Did not Solomon say: "All is vanity"?
As if the pilgrim had nothing left in his pouch.
Look: what thou canst not grasp through wisdom,
Thou would'st do well to let go.
No one should strive after the vain and the foolish —
For only what comes from the angels brings blessing.

LXIII

David, the harp player, was a poet,
Sent to bring the Psalms into the world.
The words of Virgil were both human and divine —
And I would say the same of Alighieri.

In poetry thou canst find two levels:
The entirely general one of art, then, in addition,
Genius may brilliantly proclaim itself —
Holy Words are Light from above.

LXIV

God often gives us in our earthly life
A brother-soul, who embellishes the Path,
And who, in this or that respect,
Reconciles us with the ups and downs of life.

The wise Titus Burckhardt was a friend
As there can be no better in life;
A brother, given me in far off days,
From earliest youth until the grave.

Erik von Meyenburg was a companion
Of a quite noble kind, ready for every service;
What made the nobility of his faithful soul
Even deeper, was a ray of sanctity.

LXV

The world is what it is; no more, no less.
It is but a husk; it offers itself
With all its fullness —
But in reality it is poor and empty.
Only God is That which is self-existent —
Thou findest Him in the primordial song of silence.

LXVI

Why is God "a mighty fortress,
A good bulwark and weapon"?
Because the evil one attacks us —
And gives us much to do.
Against the Wall he can do nothing —
It is the Eternal Stone;
The weapon is a ray of light
From God's Pure Being.

LXVII

Not that I indiscriminately waste time
With sentiments for animals —
But the ladybird I wish to treat with respect;
It may safely live near me.
People venerated sacred elephants,
While underestimating the smallest of God's creatures;
Thou see'st that mere size counts for little —
The tiny beetle — God led it to be honored.

LXVIII

To say Absolute is also to say Infinite;
Necessity brings with it Possibility.
The stream of things that constantly renews itself
Is nonetheless motionless above time.

A thing is what it is, but it has various modes
Of existence — not however, in terms of number;
For, when a thing has different modalities,
These harmoniously unite as one entity:

As a three-ness, a ten-ness, and so on: numbers
Thou must envision as crystals.
Multiplicity finds its happiness in identity.
Differentiation strives back towards unity.

LXIX

Vedānta and *japa-yoga*; theory and practice.
Primordial doctrine and primordial prayer —
Wisdom and invocation. The two poles
Of the soul that stands before its Creator.

LXX

If we did not suffer in this world,
The heavenly power could have no pity.
If the little child were already in Paradise,
How could the mother carry its burden?

If we were not so helpless and so little,
How could we be in God's Hands?

LXXI

Should everything be completely straight in the world?
This is a question everybody asks.
If some foolishness were not innate in us,
How could God choose the wise?

If thou wouldst seek to know what *Māyā* is —
Thou wouldst waste much of thy time.

LXXII

Once, when very young, I was alone in a forest,
And I said: "Ye Higher Powers, here I am,
I wish to be an instrument of the sacred;
Hear my prayer, and come soon."

Heaven's answer did not fail —
Had it not come, I would have written nothing.

LXXIII

Praised be the power of light
From God's Eternal Word;
The ray from the Most High's Face
Is security for my soul.

Whatever darkness may devise —
The power of Heaven breaks it.
Be still, my heart. For vain are
The noisy words of nothingness.

LXXIV

Ye have, on earth, the most beautiful house,
And suddenly, it is of the past.
Be wise, be not concerned —
In Heaven, it makes no indifference.

LXXV

Imagine there came a group of mourners;
You ask: what is it that these people mourn?
One replies with some embarrassment:
These are only people who know too much.

Then come other people, full of cheer —
What is it, you ask, that makes you so happy?
The answer: there is no wise man
Who values an excess of factual knowledge.

Knowing may be far removed from understanding —
What one cannot grasp, one should drop.

LXXVI

Do not seek enigmas in *Ātmā*'s heights —
It is *Māyā* that we do not understand.

The meaning of the world is to manifest *Ātmā* —
Let All-Possibility weave its play.

What has no beginning, will not pass away.

LXXVII

Beauty is first and foremost in nature —
Everywhere thou seest the trace of the Creator.

Then there is great human art —
In every noble work God's favor blooms.

Beauty of language: the genius of Dante
Braids a garland that links thee with God.

Music: a mystery that resounds from Heaven,
And brings the inexpressible to earth.

To the magic of music belongs the dance —
The garland of *gopis* circle round Krishna's flute.

Then there is woman: the quintessence of the beautiful —
The reconciling ray of the power of God.

LXXVIII

Man was created for eternity;
But one thing is certain: we have the right to be human —
A to-and-fro that is not easy to master.

The meaning of the human state is God alone;
Thou must find the One deep within the other —
God will forgive thee the plight of being human.

LXXIX

One calls the evil one Lucifer — wrongly so;
He never should be called "bearer of light."
Light can only be borne by what comes from the Spirit;
Truth cannot be burning in hell.

LXXX

What is from God? That which leads us to Him —
Be it direct, like knowledge and love of God;
Or indirect, like beauty,
Which we can understand in God.

LXXXI

Every prophet is "Lucifer" — in the true sense of the word,
Which means: consecrated to Light;
And it is a sin to misuse this name —
A crime against language, that cries out to Heaven.

It is said that the highest angel fell —
This is the greatest nonsense of all.
What fell was a high possibility
Which, in the grip of the devil, took itself for God.

The highest angel is like God's mirror —
His wings are made of eternal light.

LXXXII

Phosphor — bearer of light — we call the brightness
Of surfaces that shine by themselves;
It is a wise word — it bears witness to the state of grace
Of the souls that have reached light in God.

In God: the Most High created those rare souls
Who, of themselves, choose the Path to the Self.

LXXXIII

I dreamt I had a visit from Dante,
And someone said to me: do not tire him —
He is already several hundred years old;
I said: in the primordial power of the *Commedia*
Lies immortality — and God's Peace.

Never has earth sung anything more noble —
Time passes; but the song does not fade.

LXXXIV

One is not in this world for oneself, but for God.
Certainly we have the right to be human;
But do not forget that man
Has but one deep meaning: God alone.

For the human state is a path, not a soft cushion —
So let us do the duty imposed on us by God.

LXXXV

Nobility and depth are needed if we are to understand
That woman's beauty is a message
That gilds all other earthly things —
It is Heaven kissing the earth.

It is not as a poet that I wish to praise woman —
What compels me to do so is grace from Above.

LXXXVI

Sacred Scriptures in a sacred language —
What counts is not only their literal meaning;
Drink of the primordial song of God's nearness —
God knows what thy soul can understand.

LXXXVII

Consolations in the little everyday world —
What is important is not the little things they give thee;
But that, despite their triviality, we experience
Something of God's compassion.

LXXXVIII

The Creator spake: "Let there be light" —
Behold, how the Lord breaks through the night.
"And there was light." — Knowledge is
The miracle that measures the world.

LXXXIX

In the past, I considered eating almost a sin.
An elder taught me: absolutely not —
With everything given by God, thou canst
Secretly perform ejaculatory prayer.
What is written in nature
Is the work of God — and is a prayer in itself.

Everything given thee by the Hand of the Most High
Is sacred — everything thou needest in life.

XC

To fasting and to vigils say: yes and no;
Both can sanctify, but also may be of no avail.
All that one does in the Spirit is close to Heaven —
For then the heart reposes in the All-Merciful's Will.

XCI

The touchstone that the human soul
Is not overestimating itself and is not blindly inflated,
Is that it feels its own weakness —
That it goes its way in humility and wisdom.

In humility: feeling itself like a child before God;
In wisdom: seeing things as they really are.

XCII

One of the worst things in life
Is our encounter with the absurd —
It is said that, from the beginning,
The enemy has raged against Truth and Peace.

It is written: offenses must come;
But woe unto him who provokes offenses —
Whoever is not of the Truth must perish.

XCIII

The Church Fathers said it is good
That error sometimes be in the place of knowledge —
Just as light brings with it shadow,
Darkness — for its part — demands brightness.

Heresy is like a flint which,
When you strike it, produces the spark's brightness.

XCIV

Why does God's vengeance often come so late?
Why had David to cry out in the desert?
The offense may persist for a long time —
The Lord's Wrath burns in wise degrees.

God's vengeance wills not to unveil itself —
Thou see'st not the method in its fires.
The mills of God grind slowly, says a proverb,
But they grind on and on.

XCV

A psychopath can be intelligent and learned,
And pious in his way; but do not believe that
Because his psyche has limitations,
He will escape the Last Judgement.

Responsibility is possessed by everyone
Who has the capacity to think and act rightly —
Only this has weight on the scales.

XCVI

Some peoples have to live together for a very long time;
Conquerors should never seek vengeance.
Of course one does not want to lose a war,
One wields the sword — but it is not the people's fault.

If you have bad will towards a neighboring people,
The foe will soon stand at your gate.
Happy are those who, amidst the trouble of this world,
Do not break the soul's peace in God.

XCVII

The evil one wants us to doubt the Most High
And ourselves. One should never listen to him;
Ye know the fables of old —
For instance, the fox and the sour grapes.
Believe not falsehood in the garb of wisdom —
Lies that rob you of your soul.

XCVIII

God knows how and why the world goes round,
And also how it is with my soul —
How many things befell me in life;
He knows my heart. Thus I can sleep in peace.

Essential is that I remember the Lord —
That I give Him all my heart and my life.

XCIX

The false superman must exist —
He cannot put the world out of joint;
Take care that he trouble not thy thinking.
There must be someone who believes in himself
And thereby errs concerning the nature of things —
And twists his soul to self-delusion.

C

I wronged no one,
And yet I am calumniated as no other;
Why? Because I am a man sent by God,
Who brought to earth a ladder to Heaven.

CI

Divinity as Beyond-Being is impersonal;
It is personal when, as man, thou standest before It:
When thou, with needs great or small,
Entreatest thy Lord, Creator and Judge.

Thou contemplatest the Impersonal in the Intellect;
The Intellect, like What it sees, is uncreated —
It knows, from the beginning, what thou knowest not.

CII

Serenity is like a mountain top;
Certitude is the safe cavern within it;
The first requires resignation,
The second trust in God — see how the soul
Has height and depth. The source of existence
Is holy darkness here and holy brightness there.

CIII

Vairāgyānanda was the name of a Hindu sage —
"Bliss through freedom from illusion."
Blessèd the man who, in his own soul,
Has broken the wall that separates him from God's Presence.

CIV

Vairāgya — equanimity through the nearness of God;
Blessèd the man who looks on petty things from a distance.

I am in the snow on a mountain top,
And over it blows the wind's eternal song —
Everything is white and even, as far as I can see.

CV

Where is God's help after all our prayers?
Hidden like the child Moses in the bulrushes.
What is small and remote can become mighty —
On earth, the help of the Lord is ever near.

CVI

Vedānta, dīkshā, japa: this triad —
Doctrine, initiation, and path. The path whereto?
Whither all wise thought aspires —
To the One Self, to the One Freedom.

CVII

Certainly, I am only one amongst many,
And yet I am unique through the One Truth —
In one instant, I encompass the years.

The world and life are not there for mere play —
At the end of everyday life lies the miraculous.

CVIII

Life is a constantly renewed river —
Who can retain a beautiful moment?
Man has to swim as the river wishes —
He cannot keep for himself a beautiful "now."

So remain still in the proximity of the Most High —
Thy happiness lies in the deepest folds of thy heart.

CIX

My homeland is India — for already in my youth
I let myself be penetrated by the words of the Veda.
Only in the wake of Vedantic doctrine
Could I bring my own message to the world —
The Word of God, that I hear within me.

CX

Vedānta, accompanied by *japa-yoga* —
Therein lies all that Wisdom has to offer.
Happy the man who, with God's grace in the depths of his heart,
Protects this doctrine and this path.

Yatra Krishna, tatra dharma, jaya.
Where Krishna is, there is the victory of virtue —
Truth and beauty are eternal youth.

CXI

I find enlightenment where Wisdom dwells;
And I am happy, where happiness is found.
Seek in Heaven that which is enthroned in Heaven,
And wondrously combines light and warmth;
Which God has made for thy faith —
Which rewards thy soul for its fidelity.

CXII

A living creature can abstain from a thing,
Or on the other hand it can accomplish it;
It can know contentment, and also passion;
It can be intelligent, and also sing of love.

Life offers us all these ways.
The way of ways is to strive towards God —
So let His Word resound in thy heart.

CXIII

Gold, silver, bronze and iron — the four ages
Through which humanity passes. During the golden age,
There was only peace. There was nothing to dispute —
The way to conflict of opinions was still far.

During the silver age, many things were already lost —
One had to remind people of the Word of Truth.
I feel I must have been born at that time.

CXIV

Transcience — it may well be a cheerless word,
For in fact, time takes everything away.
Yet not so cheerless, because the stream of time
Can do nothing against the kernel of eternity.

CXV

One says one knows not where to turn —
But one knows perfectly well. One has faith
In him who teaches truth, virtue and beauty;
With these three, thou canst build a bridge —
Only these three make life worth living.

CXVI

Man: half animal, half angel;
As angel, he is blessed with a spark of divinity —
Thence comes his spiritual duty. A man is a man,
Not when he seeks what everybody else seeks,
But when he meets God in his heart.

CXVII

Duty is what thou doest, because it is the Good,
Not because thou fearest Judgement Day;
Whoever does not fulfill his inner law,
Is traitor to himself, and walks the path to nothingness.

Our duty is twofold: one comes from Above;
The other, God has placed in our heart.

CXVIII

It is strange how the celebration of Christmas — and with it
The Christmas tree — has spread everywhere;
Even to the Moslems, for whom this feast
Provides a wonderful image of Paradise.
The reason is that one likes to see something
That is apart from the everyday world —
One likes to return to childhood,
With its innocence and joy.

CXIX

A rosary of wonders is the world:
Firstly space, which holds it together;
Then time, which produces becoming and passing;
Then matter, and with it the power of things;
Then consciousness. And finally pure Spirit,
Which shows us the Path to the Highest Good.

CXX

Philosophers who write books
Have as a principle to exaggerate —
This is the best way to achieve originality,
And it spares the brain the trouble to be wise.
That two and two make four is too familiar —
So they say it makes five, and they say it aloud.
They think that everything lies within their grasp —
That only what they blatantly exaggerate will succeed.

Many sages wrote nothing —
But not one of them did violence to the Light;
Not one exaggerated what is right.

No sage ever misunderstood the way of truth.

CXXI

A Jewish proverb says: patience brings roses.
It is also said: everything is in God's Hands,
So all that happens is for the best —
As God wills. Let matters rest at that.

CXXII

All that is human is also relative;
So hold fast to the Divine Absolute —
From It derives what is "yes" and what is "no."
Blessed the man who drinks from the cup of Truth,
Whom God enlightens with the wine of certitude.

CXXIII

The Peace of God waits at the door of thy heart,
It waits for thee to open it with thy faith —
Thy faith which carries certainty,
And asks not about the "why" of Grace.

CXXIV

A writer must not only see his intention,
And thereby conclude that everything is in order;
If the form, the coherence, is not good,
See how the intention fails and the meaning is lost.

True speech must not be excessive;
Be exact in things both big and small.
These rules are disregarded in the East,
Because one has in mind only the deepth of the speech.

Did not Plato say that truth
Is proved by beauty — now and eternally.

CXXV

The argument of good intention is not acceptable
When a writer or artist produces something bad,
Because a good intention must be taken for granted —
One does not write or paint in order to annoy people;
What one should offer are things that make sense.
But sometimes it may happen that the best of intentions,
Despite every effort, does not find its proper expression —
To err is human. But when the king errs,
All the rest is in God's Hands.

CXXVI

Art should not repeat nature
Without showing artistry at the same time ;
The work must not resemble Creation too closely,
As if it had stolen its reality.
A work of art must reveal a human hand —
The soul must rise to the realm of symbols;
Only then can art give joy to the spirit.

One speaks of style; by means of this formal discipline
The work is raised above mere appearance —
Style is a God-willed norm.

CXXVII

When I painted the Virgin, I never thought
That my paintings should merely reflect Mary's features;
I thought of femininity as such,
Not of Jesus' Mother alone.
And likewise the Child: thou see'st him pray inwardly —
It is the devotion of all the world's Prophets.

CXXVIII

Shankara brought two things: *Vedānta*,
Which is doctrine, and *japa*, which is invocation;
The wisdom of the Veda, and the cult of the Name
That washes away all guilt from the soul.

CXXIX

The Blessèd Virgin probably had golden brown hair,
And eyes that shone with love of God;
Her lips rather full; and a grace
That no earthly hand can paint.

The name of the most beautiful flower, which I invoke —
Il nome del bel Fior ch'io sempre invoco,
Dante says in his *Paradiso*:
I saw it shine at the highest level.

CXXX

You may often keep silent about a certitude,
But if you wish to impart it, you must support it
With clear logic; for those who hear you
Want to see a meaning in what you are saying.
You must not say: I am certain of this—
And then withdraw in proud obscurity.
Finally: what is of no use to anyone,
You are not obliged to preach in the streets.

CXXXI

One kind of certitude: five and two make seven;
But another knowledge
Is what God has inscribed in our heart.
Reason and intellect: these are the two paths
Of those who, on different levels, love the Truth.

Thou canst not discover the Most High by brooding —
May He awaken Himself in the depths of thy soul.

CXXXII

Genius is good if it has a content that
Makes it a blessing here-below;
Otherwise let it be far from our world —
Better than fireworks is God's Peace.

CXXXIII

Ask if space has a limit —
It must have, and so must time;
Unimaginable is the roundness of the cosmic container
In which the magic of existence blossoms forth.

Number also appears limitless — who knows
Where, on God's command, its limit is;
For nothing created can be infinite.
The "where," the "no-further," and the "how" —
The end of possibility, God alone knows.

CXXXIV

Whence comest thou? I come from prayer.
Whither goest thou? I go to God's Will.
What wishest thou? That which is best for me —
And may the Lord fulfill whatever is pleasing to Him.

World Wheel

Sixth Collection

I

There is the beauty that we can see or hear —
Whether it be in nature or in art;
And there is beauty in the realm of thought:
In the land of poetry, in the trails of the gods.

Every spiritual consciousness
Has an element of beauty, which we can feel;
May the blessing that radiates from the Spirit
Play on the harp-strings of our soul.

II

A beginning is the beginning of an end,
And every end was once a beginning;
Whatever is in time, was first a kernel,
Then blossomed, then approached its end —
And above it stood the star of its existence.

III

Rest, purity and peace we find,
When we take refuge in the Most High.
Thus can man tame his earthly nature
With God's gracious help.

In the river Ganges, the soul is purified;
So too in God, when our soul's distress
Puts its trust in Him; it cannot be otherwise —
After dark hours blooms the rosy dawn.

IV

He who says Truth also says highest duty;
From this one come all other duties.
Whoever disregards it, loves not Truth.
Whoever calumniates others will destroy himself.

The Supreme Truth radiates from the Supreme Being.
Adherence to the True purifies the soul.
Ye will find nothing false in the Supreme Good,
So be upright in all that ye do.

V

How do we know that we have certitude?
How indeed do we know that truth is true?
No such question can be asked by a sound mind
That measures with the measures of God.

Certitude is always knowledge of certainty;
This is the Intellect. Else we are mere foolishness
That shuts its eyes to what is evident.

VI

One calls *upaguru*, whatever teaches;
Even a lady bug can be a teacher —
Or an autumn leaf, falling from a tree;
Happy the man who honors God in everything —

Who does not associate with Him another greatness
And who hears God's voice even in the smallest things.

VII

To be or not to be — that is the question Hamlet asks,
Because he knows not where to turn;
He has no solid ground beneath his feet,
So he has only one choice: to flee from his own nothingness.

Doubt comes from the realm of darkness,
It is said in the Veda; because whoever says "yes" to God
Also has certitude regarding created things.

Happy the man whose faith is like a rock.

VIII

An aristocratic type is one thing;
Another is the aristocrat as such.
The way his essence was ordained by the Creative Spirit:
Chivalrous, of noble substance,
Half-hero, half-saint, a total man —
A heart in which thy heart also can trust.

IX

The shepherd lad heard the alp-horn call —
Across to his fatherland he wished to swim;
They caught him, he never would see it again —
He would have liked to die in his mountain heights.

Had he known, without asking the world,
That we carry our homeland deep in our heart,
And that the true center never wavers,
Never passes away — he would have been thankful to God.

X

I often think of people, it could be anyone,
Whom I have seen once, and will never see again;
Not knowing why I thought of them —
We are all made of the same earth,
And pass away like shadows —
God grant that the shadows become light.

Ma già volgeva il mio disio e 'l velle
L'Amor che move il sole e l'altre stelle.

XI

You know the saga of Hero and Leander:
Nightly he swam to her across the sea,
Guided by her light. One stormy night
The light went out — he came no more.
Destiny comes and passes. Nonetheless:
You should never forget the greatness of love.

In God alone is the eternal return.

XII

"Verily, after hardship cometh ease" —
Thus it is said in the holy Koran.
If thou hast found the way to thy Lord,
The blind ice of hardship is broken.

XIII

New year — it has buried the old year
And comes with new life, new gifts,
And God's blessing. What constantly renews itself
And what, without knowing it, we possess,
Is a return from an eternal Today.

XIV

The Ten Commandments on Mount Sinaï
Were written on stone by lightning
For all times, word for word, with power,
Shaking the mountain — teaching us what to do
In order to love the Lord with our whole being.

XV

To be logical is a kind of martyrdom;
Logic often brings the intelligent man
Problems with people who will not think;
However: thou canst not be angry with too many people.

The statement that a barn is burning
Does not oblige one to explain the cause,
As many thoughtless people conclude;
It would indeed be wonderful if everyone were logical.

But: I do not want to be punctilious.
Patience; and let the sunshine in.

XVI

Certitude of God; certitude of salvation.
God alone is Reality; He will forgive.
Only He is unconditional; salvation is conditional —
But both should gladden the heart of man
If in its depths God's Grace resounds.

XVII

Can one improve one's karma?
People pray to the goddess Lakshmī for happiness.
The power of Heaven is free: in Lakshmī's hands
Is the life and destiny of all men.

Certainly, one should be resigned. But also:
The Calumet's smoke of hope ascends to Heaven.

XVIII

With the Red Indians, the miraculous
Is always "big medicine"; and the shaman
Is there to work minor miracles —
And to exhort us to the right path.

The miraculous powers of the Great Spirit penetrate
Mysteriously into all things.

XIX

He who says beauty, means also beautiful women —
For it is interiorizing to behold them:
To see Pure Beauty in femininity as such,
In a noble and loving way —
As if the soul were already in the meadows of Heaven.

XX

"One should not praise the day before the evening."
But neither should one criticize life's dream;
For whatever good thou hast woven into this dream —
God will reward thee on the Day of Judgement.

XXI

One loves the Red Indians because they were heroes;
And the Hindus because so many have been saints;
The Japanese, because they created such wonderful art;
And the Chinese, who painted gray mountain slopes —
They painted everything that was delicate, even the wind.

XXII

Persians painted charming miniatures,
And so did Hindus, to illustrate the Krishna sagas;
For minor arts must be. On the other hand,
The soul must dare to create the great:
In Agra shines the white Taj Mahal;
In Kamakura, challenging the whole world,
The Dai-Butsu towers over all.

XXIII

I saw a naked woman in a dream;
She came, walking through a field of flowers,
With floating steps, as only an angel walks.
I was a child; I asked her who she was —
"I no longer think," was the woman's reply.
She was the refuge of Beauty and Love,
This I knew. Then she took my hand,
And pulled it towards her, firmly, without shyness —
I felt I stood on holy ground;
God be praised. Then the dream was over.

XXIV

There is a thinking without images,
That takes delight in principles alone;
Then there is the realm of symbolism,
Where Truth is combined with images.
Each kind of thinking must exist in its proper place;
Different intentions require different expressions;
The essential is that the Truth should manifest Itself.

But know: a principle is also concrete —
It depends on how one understands this word.
And in symbolism too there is abstraction —
For it excludes everything extraneous.

XXV

No man has seen the edge of space,
The stream of time — who knows when it began?
It flowed out of the origin of things,
And no one knows its God-willed "when" —
The mechanism of the universe, thou wilt never understand.

XXVI

I know a Chinese girl, beautiful
And lovable, who often serves us,
For, in a restaurant, every day,
She earns her living as a waitress.

Why she looks sad — I do not know;
She scarcely speaks, I ask no questions.
I only know one thing — that I carry within me
Her deeply mysterious face.

XXVII

Say not that this or that poem is worldly,
Or that it should not have been written.
In each one there is something of the inner light —
Otherwise it would not have entered the poet's heart.

XXVIII

If Dante did not shrink from mentioning the dreadful,
It is because he had in mind the right of punishment
When the sinner had grievously offended his Lord.

As a noble man, Dante took pleasure in the beautiful —
See how his heart burned with profound longing,
And how his *Paradiso* gives us light and love.

XXIX

I call horizontal that which is merely of this world,
And vertical that which gazes into the heights of the Spirit.
Greatness is to be found in both domains —
But only the second is Heaven's bride.

Be not seduced by human greatness —
Not every genius stands before God's door.

XXX

There are three outward animal and human types:
First balanced, then light, then heavy;
This gradation does not concern our spirit —
In the spirit there is neither "less" nor "more."
However: the type can color the spirit's expression —
The word, the language, but not the content;
Every symbol allows thee to inherit the True —
So perceive the Lord in every shape.

Praise God, whose Word resounds in all forms.

XXXI

One is the number of the Absolute.
Two means male and female.
Three is the number of return to the One —
Or of manifestation, radiation, gift.

Totality — there is no explanation;
Let us be content with what we have —
To us, the uncountable should be indifferent.

XXXII

North, South, East, West — the first pattern of quaternity;
Then cold, warmth, light, and darkness;
Then reason, sentiment, imagination, and memory;
Then the Pure Intellect, which liberates us.
The powers of the soul — they are but symbols
Of the power of the Spirit, beyond all time.

XXXIII

The meaning of five — behold thy hand:
Four fingers stand opposite a fifth
Which rules them, as if it were the center;
This is a prototype, and thou see'st it again and again.

Six — in this, two and three combine;
Passivity and activity; on each side
Are three spiritual powers: Fear, Love, then Knowledge,
Which, with His grace, may lead thee to the Most High.
Two pillars with three levels:
Six ways to invoke the One Lord.

XXXIV

If in thy deepest nature thou art philosopher,
Thou canst not choose a narrow faith;
If thou findest thy happiness in fideistic zeal,
Thou canst not speak of the Pure Intellect.

Look into the fundamental content of thy heart;
God made it; but souls are different.
And different is their spiritual destiny.

XXXV

Om namo sarva Tathāgata Om —
Hail to all who walk the way "thus-gone";
Like the many who have striven towards Brahma —
They were able to attain the highest goal,
Because they did not merely think the meaning of existence,
But intensely lived it with their entire soul.

XXXVI

The spiritual message is the function of the sage,
The saint. The hero's function is the people's weal.
The duty of the honest man is honorable work.
In the case of each individual,
Duties point towards the Most High —
Whoever does not follow his calling, does not prosper.

XXXVII

The Lord is Reality and Presence —
This is That which is, the Supreme Being.
Certitude of God, along with certitude of salvation —
This is man; this alone is his path.

God is the Outward and the Inward:
I am His property, and He is mine.

XXXVIII

A noble man is one who knows himself,
And dominates himself; these are the two signs.
And if seduction or trial comes,
He will — in God — not deviate.

XXXIX

One puts the royal prince on the throne,
And places on his head the golden crown.
And then one says to him — I know not who can dare —
Now thou art king, and hast nothing to say.
This sounds highly improbable,
But this is how it is in our day.

XL

Animals are symbols — see how
The gazelles flee from the lion,
And how the lion rather avoids elephants,
Not without reason — the king becomes modest.

XLI

Forget not to think of thy Creator;
For, if thou wishest that He forget thee not,
And measure thee not with too strict measures,
Then thou must give Him thy heart and thy life.

Certainly, every day has its burden;
If thou wishest that God take account
Of what, despite thy weakness, is good in thee,
Thou must direct thy whole being towards the Most High,

So that He may break down the wall of earthly illusion.

XLII

Calumny and megalomania go together,
Because they come from the same lying spirit.

Do not believe that a small evil weighs not heavily —
The one who casually sins, sins more and more.

Truthfulness and humility open wide
The door to felicity and the Most High.

Arrogance and pride thou shouldst ever flee —
How easily God pardons a childlike heart!

XLIII

Good people give thee joy;
Bad ones thou must bear with patience
Out of love of the Lord; knowing that the world
Would not be earthly without its burdens.

Patience is gratitude at all times;
Wherever thou art grateful, there is blessing.

XLIV

Is not the Kingdom of Heaven also a world?
Whatever is a world, must have shadows;
But in Paradise, there is everywhere
The grace of God with its gifts —
Just as, after the day, the mild evening comes,
The blessing of which helps all good souls.

XLV

You imagine angels as beautiful women,
And not wrongly; but there are also
The Lord's knights, with lance, sword, and shield:
In God's Name, they look after the rights of the good.

Creatures, who are the servants of the Most High,
Are like the storm that breaks down everything —
Or like the mild and gentle wind of spring.

XLVI

One would be happy to write a poem,
But nothing happens, no inspiration comes.
One cannot force things; so one remains silent,
And is happy anyway. Patience — such is life.

XLVII

Michelangelo — was right — as a poet
To be envious, in the best sense of this word,
Of Dante's soul; for he was tired
Of suffering so long from his own soul.

XLVIII

Beatitude — it cannot last eternally,
Because God alone is eternal. Yes, but also no:
For since the holy Scripture promised us eternity,
The soul also can be beyond time — in *Ātmā*.

XLIX

What is man? He is intelligence and will,
Then character: virtuous or not;
Then destiny — what the Hindus call karma.

And after the ego comes holy silence;
The relationship with the Highest Light —
With God. May our soul come to know the Self.

L

Intelligence, reason, and pure Spirit;[1]
In French: *intelligence, raison et intellect.*
One must clearly distinguish these basic concepts —
To confuse concepts brings endless trouble.
Of course, one must honor one's own language —
However, French has much to teach us.

Germans of earlier times wrote much in Latin —
But they nevertheless remained German.

LI

"Rest in peace" — This has two meanings:
The repose of the earthly soul after death,
But above all, the repose of the faithful soul;
God grant that it choose the path Upwards.

Requiescat in Pace: this saying
Refers to what is made for immortality:
The bride of God when, in her last hour,
She awakens, blessèd, in eternal Peace.

LII

When thou thinkest of God, all is well —
When God thinks of thee, thy heart is at peace.
Wherever thou goest, thou comest closer to God —
So long as thou keepest in mind what the Most High wills.

LIII

Patience brings *báraka*, the Arabs say —
This means a blessing that radiates from the Most High;
The one who is resigned, for God, through all the pains
Of life, has paid many a debt.

LIV

Full of trust thou shouldst walk through life —
May the angels' protection accompany thee.
Bear with patience the blows of destiny —
What counts is one thing alone: love of God.

LV

It may be asked whether the elect in Heaven
Are clad in raiment, or are naked:
Both must be true, for beatitude
Must include everything that has a meaning.
Ask not "where" or "why" —
Every truth has the right to have its symbol.

LVI

Mary is called Co-Redemptrix.
One could say the same of the *Shakti*,
For her duty is joyfully to share
The burden of the *Avatāra*.

Wherever the masculine liberates souls,
The hand of the feminine cannot be absent.
The duty of man is preaching and struggle —
More existential is the way of femininity.

LVII

If thou sayest thy prayer with the right intention,
It is indifferent what evil spirits murmur —
If thou art linked to God, they cannot
Darken thy soul or thy day;
The Lord will turn thy mind to what is best.

Say: God — and this is certainly not difficult —
And the hands of the evil one will be weak and empty.

LVIII

Perhaps thou art tired of thy soul,
And thinkest thy wandering has reached its limit,
And that thy poor praying is not good —
Wake up, and be glad in faith!
Even if thou likest not thy prayer —
Well, thou must value it, despite thy weakness;
Thou owest it to the Most High — and to the world.

Happy are those who bring hope to the world.

LIX

When I was a child, other children used to ask me
For advice; then, later in life,
It was the same: I always had to
Give advice and help to others.

From my childhood, I felt within me
A certitude that was inborn
And always brought an answer.
For I was chosen to teach and to help.

There is no question here of "I" and "thou" —
In God's Will thou shouldst find thy peace.

LX

Port-Vendres, where the ship lay at anchor —
I will never forget that golden day.
I was alone in my room; the others
Wanted to walk for a while along the shore.
They had given me a bunch of flowers —
I gazed into their bright splendor
And thought, like a child, of Paradise;
Then came — a waking dream — the Virgin sweet,
And stayed with me, hidden deep within me
With her grace, which never disappeared —
Holy presence and luminous remembrance.
An image come from Heaven; I like to call it
The *Stella Maris* — my morning star.

LXI

Four seasons of the year thou bearest in thy soul;
Each one possesses its magic and its joy;
There is no question about what one should choose —
For what comes from God, leads back to Him.

Blossoming, unfolding, looking back, wise silence —
God grant that each phase may fulfill its meaning.
Childhood, youth, manhood, old age — four stages
Through which each "I" must pass.

LXII

A Formula, a Name, from a Sacred Scripture,
Painted on a panel on a wall —
Is this panel sacred, or is it
Merely ordinary wood or ordinary stone?
The material is sanctified, this is certain —
And truly sacred is the inscription's meaning.

Seek not to restrict things —
Seeing their essential content is more profitable;
May the inscription lead thee to the True.

LXIII

Maria is the *Stella Matutina*,
Because she is the early morning light in the soul —
Because she kisses my heart, which I gave to the Lord,
In prayer's eternal morning.

LXIV

I was asked how one should speak to God;
I said: canonical prayer
Is universal nourishment; then read the Psalms;
And invoke God, before whose Light ye stand —
All else is contained therein.

God Himself speaks in the deepest folds of thy heart.

LXV

If thou art a pious man, who prays faithfully,
Then take care that thou thinkest not erroneously —
And that, even in small everyday matters,
Thou remainest focused on what is true;
For it could happen that, through some injustice,
Thou couldst jeopardize thy way toward the Sovereign Good —
And that, despite all thy correct effort,
Thou reapest not the hoped-for spiritual graces.
Understand that God does not forgive all sins.

LXVI

My grandmother played old German songs
On her zither, deeply absorbed,
As if her old hands were drunk;
An image that had faded away, but has now returned.
"*Alt Heidelberg, du Feine,*" sweet dreams —
The nightingales sang in the trees.

I was witness to this fairy tale —
But my interest lay not in this land of dreams;
Other things called me — I read the Gita early —
Brahma Satyam was India's message,
And this became the melody of my deepest heart.

LXVII

The doctor said, and she was right,
That I should not overwork myself;
But what I have in mind in all my efforts
Is a homeland, deep in God's Peace.

LXVIII

Exception proves the rule;
"Let five be even" — in other words:
Legitimate irregularities
You find everywhere in this world;
And everyone knows it who examines ideas
And who, without prejudice, loves the Truth.

LXIX

The earth turns in the dark cold night —
Heaven's consolation is that the sun keeps watch
With light and warmth, bestowing power of life —
Thus has the Lord Himself entered thy soul.

What is it basically that makes us happy?
It is God, Who created the ray of selfhood;
Our "yes" to God in the kernel of our soul
Is our path, and the star of our existence.

LXX

Landscapes: meadows, forests, hills —
Mountains with eternal snow; also brooks, large rivers;
Then ponds, lakes, and the vast sea;
God grant that in the course of my life
I overlook nothing of this world's beauty —
Of all that is Mother Earth's adornment.

Where did I experience my finest hours of peace?
This may be difficult to say. However —
I found my home in a forest;
I could escape the turmoil of the world.

LXXI

It is my karma that I must, and may, be man.
Is not man the door
To the meaning of existence, and so to bliss?
God grant that the human condition lead us not astray.

God awaits us; be ye ready for Him.

LXXII

Three things are sacred to me: firstly Truth;
Then, in its wake, primordial prayer;
And then virtue — nobility of soul which,
In God, walks all the paths of beauty.

LXXIII

Primordial Truth grants you the miracle of certitude;
Never think that in your mind nothing can be certain.
From truth and certitude derives the act
Which, in the soul, rends the illusion of *Māyā*:
Namely quintessential prayer; then the heavenly realm
Of virtue — nakedness and raiment both at once.

LXXIV

There is a vengeance that comes from passion;
Then there is one that comes from justice.
"Revenge is sweet" — because the evil one wants it;
And then, because wickedness cries out to Heaven.

LXXV

Rectitude: observe moderation in everything;
Only the slave of passion is immoderate;
Whatever is true, thy spirit need not obtain by force.
God knows, so it is said, what is in our breast —
With God's measures, the work may succeed.

But there is a question thou shouldst not forget:
Is not the pure love of God measureless,
The love that frees thee from the world's vain turmoil?
Certainly: thou canst not measure what is infinite.

LXXVI

Man may regret many false steps,
And grieve over his sins and the flotsam of his soul —
He may, before God, bend his proud knee,
And with shameful breast lie in the dust;
The final word will be his faith —
The heart's hope for eternity.
How many, thinking themselves worthless,
Have, through God's grace, risen to the Light.

LXXVII

Two paths: quintessential Truth and quintessential Prayer;
Two gifts: God with thee, and Marian grace.
One word: let not thy self be troubled —
And let the wheel of the world's events turn.

LXXVIII

There were powers, from childhood onward,
Which sought to destroy thee; they could not succeed.
In every trial, help was there;
In the darkness, thou couldst hear the angels' singing.

LXXIX

A German heart — depth and poetry;
Then comes, by destiny, the Latin element.
But the deepest kernel of my heart, by vocation,
Is *Brahma Satyam* — the Vedantic spirit
Which was the first in Creation.

These are, from God, my dimensions.
Not that I think here of profound poetry—
An intermezzo can also be justified.

LXXX

If thou wishest, in this world, to speak of the True,
Thou must take into account the wicked and the insolent,
Who, *Deo gratias*, can achieve nothing —

For *vincit omnia Veritas.* God, who is power,
Takes the end into His Hands.

Say to thyself: whatever thou wishest in the Lord will succeed.

LXXXI

Folk-songs are often songs of longing.
It is as if in the evening, after the day's work
Or perhaps following a feast, the tired peasants
Wished to be moved in honor of the beautiful and the holy.
The nature of the people is not simply love of life;
Nobility lies within each honest breast;
As do much love and much sorrow, some might add —
Everyone must bear the burden of being human.

LXXXII

A phenomenon of old age:
Things long past come back into the space of mind
Whether one wishes it or not; God grant that all
Illusion be dissoved in the incense of prayer.

For experience has long taught us
That we can never be more happy
Than when our spirit finds itself in God —
Without vain melodies from bygone days.

LXXXIII

The saying *ora et labora* comprises
Everything that is essential in life:
Firstly the meaning of existence, and then
What thou must do in order to earn thy living.

It is often said that work is prayer —
Nonsense; if thou couldst make a living
Without work, and devote thyself only to prayer,
Thou wouldst have one foot in eternal life.

LXXXIV

"Late ye come, but come ye do," said a poet
In a play; this is often quoted.
"Better late than never" — a saying that means:
Happy the man who loses nothing,
Because he comes, though at the last hour;
A saying that comforts those who come late.

Therefore, people, be not discouraged,
If ye do what is right at the last moment.
Nevertheless: to postpone would be poor advice —
One never knows if one will still have time.

LXXXV

Rothenburg, Dinkelsbühl: dream-filled cities
In Franconia — streets still redolent
Of olden times; places where I would have
Gladly remained longer than in fact I could.

Now my home is far from urban happiness:
A virgin forest in the legendary West,
Chosen by the Lord in a new world.

God knows best what befits my innermost nature —
He who enlightens my heart with His grace.

LXXXVI

Take care to use expressions that make sense —
One can only approve what is faultless.
"May God continue to give you His grace" —
Write not thus; therein lies something discordant —
For there is no reason to think
That what God has given us is uncertain.
"I pray that your journey be good and happy" —
This implies: if I do not pray, perhaps there will be
A hurricane, and your ship will sink.
"May the Lord enlighten you" is a tautology
When reason is sufficient and there is no problem.
See how so many people, with the best will,
Choose the wrong kind of rhetoric.

LXXXVII

There are three spiritual worlds to which I belong:
The primordial world of the Veda, then Sufism,
And then, in the West, the world of the Indians;
Each branch of humanity has something to teach,
For every cosmos shines in its own way.
Metaphysics means the words of the Vedas;
The Name of God is the world of the Sufis;
And our harmony with surrounding creation
Is what pleases the heart of the Indian.

LXXXVIII

I grew up amid the sounds of the violin —
I know many old melodies,
More than I wish; I would often like to flee
To the land of silence and of the gods.

But both are meaningful — Heaven's sounds
And Heaven's silence. Let beauty sing —
And then, if another hour so wish,
Let it in Being — in the ungraspable — fade away.

LXXXIX

Let two graces enter thy heart:
Transparent Beauty and Pure Being.
In the beautiful, said Plato, the true is shining —
Their combination is the wonderful.

The beautiful should be transparent for you —
This means that it should not remain outward or sensual.
God, who wishes to show you His ways,
Will inscribe His intention into your heart.

XC

Harp and zither, lute and song;
Language of the soul, sounds of olden times —
God grant that we become music in our heart;
Then there would no longer be evil on earth.

XCI

If Plato had always been the light for everyone,
Our dark world would have recovered long ago.
Had all the world known Shankara,
Wisdom would long since have burned up illusion.

XCII

If God had willed that only good exist,
The dream that is creation would be past.

All-Possibility: this is the great word;
God put every thing in its place —

And so the melody of existence burst forth.

XCIII

Thou must hold fast to the Absolute —
What comes thereafter is in the hands of the Most High;
Whoever trusts in God, and so helps himself,
Also helps his neighbor, in the grace of the Lord.

No greater good is granted to man
Than piously to bestow God's Peace.

XCIV

"They have no wine" — these were the words
Of the Holy Virgin, who wished to give our soul to drink:
It was her loving wish to give to the sinner's heart
Something of the wine of Heaven.

"The Lord is with thee" — these were God's words,
Intended to lead us to holy trust.

XCV

The morning dawns — the new day is here.
What will happen? Do not ask this question;
Say: God; and the essential has been done.

There is nothing else, only the torment of universal illusion —
Even though the Lord may send thee many consolations;
If only the meaning of thine existence be fulfilled —

That one carry Paradise in one's heart.

XCVI

"Light upon light," it is said in the Koran;
What is the first light, and what is the second?
Nūr 'alā nūr — there is the light in the heart,
And there is the light in the Divinity's vastness.

"Truth has come, illusion has vanished" —
The sword of foolishness breaks in the final battle.

XCVII

A broken toy is on the table;
The little child cries over nothing. What happened?
This or that — but very soon,
Even for the child, the illusion will pass,
And he will laugh at his foolishness.

Thus should ye too awaken to reality!

XCVIII

Being beautiful is one thing, procreating is another;
Do not think that the second is the reason for the first.
Certainly, God wishes humanity to survive;
For God, a thousand years are but an hour.
Beauty has a purpose in God's plan —
More than the purpose is that beauty can shine.

XCIX

The *vaishya* caste in India has three degrees:
The artist, the merchant, and the man
Of superior craftsmanship. However, the wise man's spirit
Is present in all three vocations.

The *kshatriya* is a warrior or a king —
The trivialities of this world are of little concern to him.
The *brahmin* deserves the highest honor —
For he represents the Lord and His doctrine.

C

Two things the Lord can give to man:
Help and consolation. Help comes
From without; consolation from within.
To what must be, thou must be resigned,
If thou wishest — in God — to gain life's crown.

CI

People who firmly believe in voices
That come from the evil one, are not therefore bad;
Certainly, they have no gift of discernment —
But otherwise, God willing, they may be good.

One must banish credulity
And gain a firm hold on the True.
From Heaven come the strong words of Light —
What cannot come from Above, is nothing.

CII

Joy in the beautiful is not worldliness —
In the beautiful one can see God's intention
If one penetrates to the essence of things.
Happy are those who, ever ready to see things in depth,
In all their thoughts stand before their Creator.

CIII

The noble, well-shaped woman is not merely one image
Of Divine harmony amongst many others;
She is the image in itself,
To which God has given the grace of likeness;
She is not a form that can be compared;
She is the one *Māyā*, eternally —
The one primordial image, and the one She.

CIV

Thou canst not put silence into words —
Thou canst not speak of the inexpressible.
The soul would like to sing of that which has no limit —
But thou must leave this song to the Most High.

CV

Sleep is healthy — we need it here-below,
Because life makes us weary. However,
Sleep is not enough — when we have to rest,
It should be in the Peace of the Most High.

CVI

St. Louis, king of France, was playing ball with his princes.
If thou hadst but one day to live,
One asked, what wouldst thou do?
I would give all my goods to the poor,
Was one reply. Another said:
I would enter a monastery. But thou, O King,
What wouldst thou do? — I would play ball.

The King, free from the bondage of illusion,
Stood at all times before His Lord.

CVII

A Master cannot have a veil over his mind,
And be unable to understand men;
He would very much like to see goodwill —
He stands serene above the petty.

He does not scold lightly, for he is patient;
He knows: whoever struggles, is not guilty of sin —
Weakness is in human nature,
So let each one fulfill his duty;
This was, before God, the first man's oath.

According to the Koran, God said to the first man:
"Testify that I am the Lord" — and the man
Testified. Then came the Fall;
Not only for Adam — because the dark trace
Of the first sin thou see'st everywhere.

CVIII

It is satanic to take the good for the bad
And the bad for the good. For satan equals inversion;
Not always, if the error is superficial —
Or in the intoxication of religious zeal.

Diabolical is a God-forsaken world
That considers only earthly dross important.

CX

Life should not, for thee, be like a picture-book
Whose pages thou turnest thoughtlessly like a child;
For the everlasting thou art made —
So be not blind to what God has willed.

There is the Eye of the Heart which, within thee,
Sees the essential, the Divine One.
Happy is he in whom, if God wills,
Dwells the One Wisdom that does not fade away.

CXI

There must somewhere be a golden land,
Towards the sunset in the vast sea,
And with eternal spring.
It must be so, for this tale I hear in my heart.

CXII

Is it not a solace that — whatever we do —
We go towards God? Life is movement —
But whither? On this, thou must ponder, day by day;
Only in the Great One is there Peace.

From the Creator thou comest, and to Him thou goest;
May He give thee, hour by hour, the grace to be
What thou must be — in order to be man,
And more than just a man. *Allāh karīm.*

CXIII

I was a fabric designer in Paris;
My comrades came from Alsace;
I was content, but I dreamt much,
Until I rent this miserable little corner of happiness

And fled to Algeria — to obtain
What my longing sought; and praise be to God —
The Shaikh al-'Alāwī said: it is good that thou hast come —

From him I received the light of the Path.

CXIV

In Mostaghanem I was told
That Allah has ninety-nine Names,
Names of the essence, and of the qualities;
They are the framework of enlightenment and prayer.

God is the Loving-Kind; whoever names Him thus,
And trustingly invokes Him with this Name,
Hopes all the more that God, who knows us all,
Will be disposed to hear him. *Yā Latīf!*

CXV

What is artificial is contrary to nature.
It will be objected that, in the last analysis,
The artificial too bespeaks the workings of Nature —
Since everything comes from God's Hands.

This is true, but it does not prevent
The artificial from contradicting the authentic —
The universe wants to manifest both degrees.

CXVI

"A demolisher of everything" is what one calls a fool
By the name of Kant, who believed that what he
Called intelligence or reason, was his own work —
He thought he had discovered the limits of thought.

A consolation against the straw of such philosophers
Is that there are always flames in the fireplace.

CXVII

The word "philosopher" has two meanings:
Firstly, the meaning that it had before Descartes;
And then the absurdity of the moderns:
A thinking that operates only with reason.

If one wishes to measure with true measures,
One should not forget what is said here.
A philosopher is any man who thinks,
Including the sage who never violates the Truth.

CXVIII

In the prophetic man, there are two poles:
Thinking and Being — the words of his message,
And the radiation of his substance;
Each pole has its wisdom in its proper place.

Truth and beauty; or light and love;
Inspiration of the True, and noble instincts.
Shankara, who proclaims the Lofty Message,
And Krishna, who winds the garland of *gopis*.

CXIX

What can one do, if one wishes to obtain salvation
But knows no Path or Method;
Or if, for one reason or another, one is not part of
A recognized spiritual school?

If one cannot do otherwise — I would advise:
Ceaselessly repeat a verse from the Psalms,
Do what is good, and abstain from what is forbidden —
Thou wilt be saved, on this thou may'st rely.

Pride must never be in our attitude;
Walk in God, if thou wouldst walk alone.
It is no sin to live on the edge of the world —
There have always been hermits.

CXX

If thou hast in mind the most beautiful melody —
It may be that thou thinkest in vain of thyself,
Or it may be that this melody raises thee to the heavenly spheres,
To teach thee something of the Highest Self.

CXXI

As far as possible one should be on guard against the psyche —
Not when the Spirit penetrates it from above,
But when the soul is an end in itself,
And drowns in its own nothingness.
In the most diverse of realms, one can see
That only the radiation of the Spirit brings good.

CXXII

One can experience the beautiful like a thief;
Nobly experienced beauty is the True!
If thy soul does not strive towards the Inward,
The most beautiful thing in the world will give thee nothing.

CXXIII

"The Lord is my shepherd, I shall not want" —
"Commit thy ways unto the Lord";
So may the Most High help me
To put my body and soul into His Hands.

CXXIV

I was sent a book on Eckhartshausen;
Like other theosophers of his time,
He combined knowledge and faith very well.
He found the Path of alchemy —
Forms of the Spirit and of Infinity.

CXXV

There are principles that I constantly repeat,
Because they belong to the sage who is without fault.
First comes the doctrine concerning God;
Then the invocation of the Highest Name,
Which purifies and liberates the heart;
Then comes the beauty of all virtue, nobility of soul;
And finally the sense of forms, inward and outward.
These are the four principles —
God grant that they be never violated.

CXXVI

What is the sense of forms? That one understand
What the shape of everything means;
Every form has something to say —
The noble form wills to transmit light from Heaven.
Form and content: the latter justifies the former;
Form incarnates what I long for —
Just as the sun's chariot strives toward the heights.

CXXVII

Thou art my God, and I call on Thee —
I invoke Thee, who art the Lord.
My spirit is near Thee in the Eternal Now —
In the Light, which is beyond time.
I used to say: "I am small, my heart is pure" —
Already as a child I wished to be with Thee.

CXXVIII

How should we encounter the Divine?
As man or as child? Certainly in both ways.
And may God, with His grace-filled Hands,
Bless all that we are capable of being.

As man: if we aim toward the Highest Truth;
As child: if we feel poor and helpless —
For one needs God on all levels of the soul.
One thing alone is needful — that we invoke Him with faith.

World Wheel

Seventh Collection

I

Nothing on earth can be better
Than a heartfelt, inward prayer —
Be it only a single word
That never passes away.

Were there but one person in the world
To think of the Most High —
It would be more than if one gave
Thee the whole of the Alhambra.

II

If one had made it difficult for someone
To find repose in the grace of prayer —
It is as if, in the night, one had stolen
The best from him — yea, his very soul.

An angel comes down to earth and looks to see
If somewhere there is a call to Heaven —
If someone here below forgets not the Lord;

For the All-Merciful is waiting, so that with the treasure
Of His Graces, He may bend down towards earth.

III

What is the meaning of the Name of God?
Firstly, Reality; then the Presence of the Real;
And finally, the word of the soul
That hopes for liberation.
The Name of God is the best place.

IV

A beautiful maiden came and asked me:
What is the miracle of liberation?
I told her: it is the substance of Beauty
In thy heart. Be faithful to thyself.

This is a symbol — for I did not say it;
Yet it is true — I say it in the poem.

V

Wert thou not a poet, thou wouldst be a philosopher;
Wert thou not a philosopher, thou wouldst be a poet;
The Creator gave thee a nature
Which of itself follows both paths.

Both paths: thou canst find them
Wherever the true and the beautiful combine to become one —
Where the spirit of the great Plato blows.
The priestess Diotima taught Plato love,
And Plato taught wisdom to the whole world —
See how the wisdom of Eros miraculously
Joins with the highest spiritual knowledge.

VI

Snow White, Little Red Riding Hood, and the Sleeping Beauty —
Ye think they are idle fairy tales;
But the treasury of fairy tales stems from olden times —
And has a deep wisdom to teach you.

Symbols — ye carry them within you;
He who is wise will willingly listen to them.

VII

In the past I believed eating to be almost a sin,
And I fasted, and became ill.
However: what is necessary for life, is pleasing to God;
Whoever acts with proportion is free from all sin.

VIII

Snowflakes whirl down to earth —
In warm homes, people sing summer songs.
In summer, when the sun burns fiercely,
They anxiously cherish everything that is cool.
Yin-yang — what does the symbol mean?
A to-and-fro — so it is with people
And with the soul. From each pole,
You should always take something of the other.

IX

One should perceive the logical and the beautiful,
Not only in great, but also in little things;
Even in the to-and-fro of daily life, we should
Prepare the way for God's blessing.
One often thinks that little is nothing —
But everything has meaning before the Face of God.

X

Objectivity — holding fast to the thing
That has its own existence apart from ourselves.
And with it comes the holy radiation of the heart —
Something of ourselves; the Lord, in His Compassion,
Watches faithfully over our selfhood.

Hold strictly to that which is as such;
Pay thy debt to realities;
Forget not that thou too art real —
God knows thee. With the world, be patient.

XI

Wisdom, poetry, music and beautiful women —
With them, I can build a bridge
To the kingdom of Heaven, and not feel forsaken;
Who can grasp the wonders of the All-Merciful?

XII

Metaphysics has two derivatives:
Firstly, knowledge of the world — cosmology —
Which has its source in the universe;
Then knowledge of the soul — psychology.
Cosmology concerns the world as "thou";
Psychology, as "I"; and metaphysics
Looks towards the Uncreated and Eternal.

XIII

I know not who invented the dance of the veils;
The veil is the Word, the body is Being.
Unveiling means: the path from illusion to Reality —
Brahma satyam; jagan — the world is appearance.

XIV

Reality — you must see two meanings here;
Firstly: the Absolute alone is real;
Secondly: what certainly has existence,
Is not pure nothingness — this is evident.

XV

Relativity — a rigorous word;
That which can be either more or less,
Either bigger or smaller, and so on —
What is it? Beyond compare is the Lord alone.

XVI

Dream-veil life — who has woven thee
And brought thee into the day of existence?
Who has conceived thy dance, thy being —
Who has kindled the soul's temporality;
Who has spun the threads of thine illusion?

Dream-veil ego — who has made thee thus,
As the Self wills? I know not;
Yet I know well that dreams must be —
Life is cosmic poetry.

XVII

O Gypsy, who standest dreaming at the door:
Let me hear a song from thy violin —
Let it talk of dance and love and suffering,
And evoke for us the vast land of the Puszta;

Let us understand why thou art restless,
And wanderest to the rim of the unknown.
May Wisdom touch thy soul —
Mayst thou find repose in the depths of thy heart.

XVIII

Dream-castle world — who built thee?
They complain that thou art full of rifts,
Forgetting thy deep meaning. Happy the man who
Trusts in the Lord despite the flaws.

Architect God — Thou knewest Thy plan;
To criticize it is the madness of fools.
All the more so in that he who complains
Does not always look to his own virtue.

XIX

There is a first pair: man and woman;
And then a second: face and body.

On the other hand, there is a ternary:
Face, breast, and sexual parts;
Which mean wisdom, beauty, and love,
Given by God; powers and beatitudes.

One could also say that wisdom is one thing,
And beauty, along with love, is the other;
God grant that we walk on our way with each of these graces.

XX

Jesus, Mary, Joseph — between the two,
The God-man and the carpenter,
Is Mary, of dual nature;
The most marvelous woman ever seen by human eye —
Always walking in the wake of the Most High.

XXI

Jakob Böhme thought that evil
Is already contained in God. Certainly not as evil,
But because All-Possibility wills it;
In God Himself, all is pure and silent.

XXII

Erwin von Steinbach, who built the Strassburg Cathedral,
Dreamt that he floated through the space
Of the cathedral, with an angel
Holding gently his hand; and he felt as though
He were not dreaming. — A bygone age, seven hundred years ago,
An age of the miraculous and the nearness of Heaven,
When no wall separated stone from Spirit —
When the angels were still our helpers.

XXIII

Play for me thy violin, sing a song
Of olden times, and I will write it down;
The gentle sound of strings can be enough
To make spring bloom in my soul.

XXIV

I often think of the past —
I drink wine from an ancient tankard.
I could break it, for I know
That in the present, I have enough.

For, when the "now" is in God's Hands,
Yesterday and tomorrow are both good.
Be happy if ye know not too much —
And if ye drink new courage from the Eternal Now.

XXV

It was in the Wild West. An Indian
Said to me: "See that white man —
I heard he is an Italian;
So go and speak to him!"
I went to him and gave him my hand:
"*Nel mezzo del cammin di nostra vita...*"
He thought I was a friend from his country.
"*Mi ritrovai per una selva oscura,*"
Was his reply. — I would never have thought
That the Wild West would bring forth the spirit of Dante!

XXVI

I wonder where my true homeland is;
Is it on the Rhine, where I was born —
Is it Mother India, which renewed my heart?
So many things led me back to the Center —
And to the beatific vastness of the Absolute.

XXVII

Freemasonry — if only it had remained
What it was at the beginning,
Much less superfluous matter would have been written;
Nevertheless: the mason builds as he can.

Stonemasons were formerly initiates,
The builders' lodges were their sanctuaries;
There they worked to build the cathedral;
There they stood before the door of Mystery.

XXVIII

The palingenesia of the soul is
Performed by the hand of the Master of Mysteries —
Either by initiation, or from within,
By the Grace of God which destroys all illusion.
Being reborn in the Spirit — a teaching from primordial times.
The Lord grant that the heart be converted.
Some come into the world with this grace —
God places Prophets along the way.

XXIX

"The next world is better for thee than this one,"
Says the Koran. One knows it, yet one knows it not;
What is on the other side, one cannot clearly see —
But one knows that the here-below will soon be broken;

Those who stand piously before the Most High
Know that the Lord has promised salvation;
One day the earthly world will no longer exist —
"But My words will not pass away."

XXX

Serenity: the soul abstains
From all dreaming about things.
Complementary to this is act: only one thing resounds
In the heart, the Presence of the Most High.
Then there is peace that calms all agitation:
Resignation to what is written.
Then certitude, that fills the spirit:
Love of the deep, inward life of Truth.

And finally there is the mystery of Oneness:
Absolutely real is the Lord alone.
The complementary pole is Selfhood:
Beyond all concepts is the silence of my real Being.

XXXI

Dream-veil soul — who has willed thee,
That thou shouldst float through earthly existence,
Renewed by image after image, by sound after sound —
That thou shouldst weave thine own existence for thyself?

Dream-veil soul — who has made thy journey,
Such that, with joy and sorrow, thou shouldst wander through life,
And — may God help thee! — strive toward the Sovereign Good.

Happy the man, in whose soul an angel sings.

XXXII

Ye think I was born on the green Rhine —
Ye know not the place of my birth.
I myself knew it not — till one day
The Most High spoke: be what thou truly art!

XXXIII

What art thou? German — also somewhat French,
Then also Arab — and finally Indian,
By adoption into the circle of the tribe.
Thus did the goddess of destiny cast her lots —
Thou knowest not how, for the Lord alone knows.

Also Mother India didst thou early encounter —
She blessed thee with the light of Wisdom.

XXXIV

Treasure-house heart, who opened thee for me —
Who bestowed new light to the darkness?
Blessèd art thou if God has revealed to thee what thou art —
And if thy heart's beat finds its end in Him.

XXXV

One of the modes of wisdom is Mastership:
The teaching function comes from God's power.
The Master's mission is difficult: he must
Give the disciple what is beneficial for his spirit;
Yet his function is also easy, thanks to God —
The duty of giving constitutes the Master's life.

God's Will is the star of his existence.

XXXVI

It is still winter, the woods are bare;
The air is cold, the sun's ray wan;
But the blackbird's song makes us think of spring —
O coming of spring, be not too long!
Yet one thing keeps me from being discouraged:
I carry in my heart eternal spring.

XXXVII

Isis — a name for All-Possibility;
For she is "all that ever was, that is,
And that will be" — but beyond all time.

"And no one can lift my veil" —
Her naked body is eternity.

XXXVIII

Immortality — whoever has grasped it
Is delivered from all burdens of the soul.
If thou knowest what becoming and passing away are,
Thou art in the pure, uncreated Spirit —
For thou hast found in God thy very being.

Beyond the idle to-and-fro of things
There is a God-willed return
To what in God thou wast before —
And mayest thou read it in thy heart.

XXXIX

O earthly wanderer, thou wouldst like to be happy —
Thou canst be, only if thou submit to God
And trust in Him; so prove that thou
Lovest Him in all thy poor ways.

XL

Resignation to God's holy Will,
Then trust in His great Goodness —
So that the weak man, on his path,
Guard himself faithfully against all that is alien to God.

XLI

The law of thinking: on the basis of truth
Proclaim the nature of things to thyself and to the world.

Happy the man who walks in the paths of the Most High —
A pure heart is eternal prayer.

XLII

"Culture" is unnecessary knowledge of too many things —
The one who writes can scarcely avoid this luxury.
Who would wish to be the servant of vain things?
One is resigned to it — one must endure it.

But who can measure where the limits are?
Wisdom has many forms; thus it is also
What the working of our mind sometimes needs —
An alternating play: remembering and forgetting.

XLIII

One often needs more courage in earthly life;
If thou knowest not what to do, be ready
To give new strength to other human beings —
The example of thy resignation to God.

XLIV

In life there is a law: whatever gives pleasure
Must, on the one hand, be natural in itself,
And, on the other, be interiorizing, and linked with the Spirit;
For the Spirit makes pure.
Human nature is multifarious —
A noble person is he who transcends it.

XLV

Remembering and forgetting — knowest thou well
What these words mean for thee?
Thou must not cling to past pleasures —
Thou must grant the world thy God-remembrance.

XLVI

Pleasure is harmless for us human beings
When it is linked with a sense of God;
When we find in that which could seduce us,
A little path towards the Truth of the Most High.

XLVII

Metaphysics, and with it the method —
Doctrine, and prayer of the heart: the two poles
Of the way to the goal. I have often said this —
God forgive me for saying it again.

XLVIII

He who has absorbed the Word of God in his heart
Is like a river — before him lies the vast sea.
And if piously thou hast reached the final shore,
Thank God — and ask no more.

XLIX

Say not that Truth is only there for thinking —
It is for living, beyond all time;
It gives thee all that thy heart can desire —
In each word of God there is beatitude.

L

The Veda: *Brahma satyam, jagan mithyā* —
In Islam: *lā ilāha illa 'Llāh.*
Māyā is all that thou see'st around thee —
Only *Ātmā* was there before Creation.

LI

The One is Creator; the multiple is world —
A teaching come from Heaven since the earliest of times.
And even had it remained hidden within the Most High —
It is written in the hearts of men.

As God proclaimed from the mountain-top:
Adonai Elohenu, Adonai Ehat.

LII

When truths are presented in a mathematical way,
Not they, but their tone, may weary us.
One might prefer — and they merit it —
To clothe them in the garment of celestial songs.

Wisdom's gaze sees the nature of things;
Thou askest: of what substance is the sage?
God made him of Intellect and music.

LIII

To be "intellectual" is not sufficient,
For noble disposition pertains to the human state;
Understanding sublime doctrine is not everything —
Only nobility constitutes the soul's total worth.

What I am saying is self-evident —
However: prejudices should be condemned.
And the scale of all values is with God alone.

LIV

There is a painting by the artist Feuerbach
Which portrays Dante with the noble women of Ravenna,
Who followed him lovingly,
To gaze upon the light of his wise spirit.

The nobility of the painting deserves praise,
Because it moves the pious man who thinks of Dante
Sì come rota ch'igualmente è mossa —
From the outward to the depths of the heart.

LV

If only the wayfarer could understand
That the hereafter is better than the here-below,
As all holy scriptures emphasize —
God grant that we measure with their measures!
For faith is not only a rigorous duty —
It is above all the desire of our heart.

LVI

There are sayings that compel us to reflect:
"God has cursed everything on earth,
Except God-remembrance and the things that
Favor it" — Mohammed's words
Are like a sword, but they are also meant to be consoling,

For everything in this world will pass away,
Except the values which reside in God,
And which already here on earth convey His blessing.

LVII

The *a priori* of all activity
Is *vacare Deo.* Without God,
One is never prepared for death.

Vacare Deo: to be empty for the Most High —
To be before God what the Lord requires of us;
Nothing better canst thou be for thy neighbor.

LVIII

The first time I saw gypsies
Was in a cellar at night.
They had come out of their wagon,
And had brought their violins.

They played *csárdás* after *csárdás*,[1]
And I thought to myself, a new life is beginning for thee,
So deeply did the violins' drunkenness affect me —
All that had happened before seemed to melt away.

LIX

Cossacks came one day, long ago,
From their distant land.
One would have loved to hear their horses' galloping —
They sang as if they were on horseback

With lance, saber, and swinging whips;
With manly singing, in deep bass voices —
Had one encountered them on the steppes,
One might not have felt much at ease.

LX

The mentality of most people is horizontal —
It should be vertical, from world to God;
It was for this that the human soul was created:
To stand before God in an eternal "today."

For we are here in order to look Upwards —
And to build a way for ourselves and others.

LXI

Think not that God owes thee special help,
Simply because thou art what thou art — whether great or small,
God helps thee how and when He will;
The infant Moses lay care-free in the bulrushes —
Thou too couldst be a little Moses.

LXII

One would like to be always agreeable and peaceful —
But one cannot, because people are too bad.
One must not spoil the average man —
Only he who keeps this in mind is just.

LXIII

Life is earnest — have no doubt;
But this is not the sole lesson of existence.
For after rigor, the heart needs music —

What would the world be, if there were no love.

LXIV

What would the harp of life be, if its sound
Were not attuned to God's goodness?
God grant that our soul's song
Be not deprived of Heaven's violins;
Happy are those whose deepest song of longing
Emerged from God's grace before their very existence —
Just as the body of the goddess emerged from the sea.

LXV

Understand: with faith comes peace,
And with trust comes resignation;
With certitude comes serenity —
The most beautiful strains from the same song.

Let thy heart be conscious of this at all times.

LXVI

The greatest spirits never regretted
To have sung of wisdom and love;
Wisdom was for the monasteries,
And love, for the noble troubadours.
Thus, in ancient times, every song, every melody,
Found its place to gladden the earth —
Let us say that love, as lived by the sage,
Teaches you how to feel and what to do.

LXVII

Expansion is continuous
When a spiral flows outwards —
And it is discontinuous
In the case of concentric circles:
The first is movement, the second is rest;
Behold how complex is the structure of space.
Such is our ego with its rhythms —
Eternally immutable is *Ātmā* alone.

LXVIII

If thy soul feels unwell, say "yes" to God —
In the "yes" to God is the best remedy.
In the Name of God, thou feelest secure,
Whatever thy tired soul's pain may be.

In the Name — think not that the Path is far.

LXIX

What will the world be like thousands of years from now?
Who knows what the earth's forms were in the past?
There one should ask the scientists.

We are apprehensive, not only of transience,
But also of change — no one knows
Where the mountains or the seas once lay.

LXX

Thousands of years ago — who can know
Whether our region was hot or cold?
No one is in a position to find out —
And if one could, one would be sore afraid.
Wanderer, go thy way intent on thy duty —
Wonder little about the unthinkable,
And leave to God what we cannot know.

LXXI

A sage is one who combines Truth and Beauty,
And bases both on the Being of the Divinity.
He is not wise who only sees the half,
And flees from ultimate conclusions.

He is wise who measures with God's measures,
And knows that in his heart dwells That which is —
That which the spirit powerfully draws inwards.

LXXII

A dull day: joy had ebbed away;
And yet a bright day: it was found in God.
For it often happens that when good comes to thee,
Evil threatens with its seed of poison.
Thus a bad beginning is often a sign
That angels will soon reach out their hands to thee.

LXXIII

Thou mayest wonder, when vexation overtook thee,
Why destiny has taken away thy happiness;
It is often — and thou must ponder this —
Because the Most High wished to give thee an experience;
Know that experience is a precious good —
So accept it, in God, with a joyful mind,
And let thyself be led on the path to the Best.

LXXIV

The Shaikh Al-'Alāwī was first an 'Isāwa[2] —
He played his flute and charmed snakes.
Shaikh Bu Zidi came to him and said:
Enough! This is a vain activity;
Choose between the false and the true —
Put away thy flute and tame thy soul.

LXXV

Why is the soul full of vain images,
When its happiness lies in the Great One.
Happy is he to whose soul, in the night,
The blessing of the Supreme Name has come;
Whom God's Grace cradles into deep contemplation —
Who thought of God — and of whom God has thought.

LXXVI

Sadness comes to us from nature,
But bitterness comes from the evil one.
Man may often be deeply grieved —
Whoever becomes bitter, should be ashamed before God.

LXXVII

I would like to define six summits among man:
First, I mention the prophet,
Who has received a message from God,
In the wake of which a sector of humanity lives.
Then I mention the saint — his example
Is our shield against evil powers.
Then I praise also the sage,
Without whose spirit the world cannot live.

And then the hero, powerful in the warrior's state —
His sword guarantees security in the land.
Then too the genius, creator of noble art —
He rightly receives the admiration of many ages.
And finally, there is the good man, of simple type,
His presence is of great worth.

LXXVIII

So many things that we call earthly
Have brought to earth something of Heaven;
People think that man invented the beautiful —
But it came of itself, to manifest the Divine;
It is not wholly made for our world.

Behold the headdress made of eagle feathers —
A god has bowed down towards the earth.
Forms that link us to the eternal —
No man on earth could have devised them by himself.
The eagle headdress, image of majesty —
In the beginning, it was an angel's raiment.

LXXIX

It can happen that in a poem
One chooses a wrong expression — something exaggerated,
Or unclear; the thoughts may skip
From one meaning to another —
But the essential has remained intact.

LXXX

Certainly, life is not an easy path —
Destiny has sown it with thorns;
But I have no choice, I must go on —
If I do not continue, it is time that will continue.

And yet there is something stronger than the dream:
The Absolute, which dwells within the heart,
And which, God willing, vanquishes time —
If It radiates for thee, life scarcely counts.

Think of the Day of Divine Judgement —
Say "yes" to God, and be not troubled.

LXXXI

Be thou aware that only the One is —
Earthly *Māyā* is the great void.
In essence, thou art not other than the One —
This is the doctrine, ever since God created the world.

LXXXII

Thou shouldst not despise small joys;
God gives them to accompany the great ones.
Joy is a ray from the kingdom of Heaven —
God wished to prepare a feast for thee.

LXXXIII

The wise man's heart is like the Ark of the Covenant —
A shrine for God; no man can measure this grace;
What is manifested outwardly thou canst measure,
But God's freedom thou must never forget —
The inward Path is limitless, and straight.

Shekhīnāh — God's presence, which dwells within thee,
Which has its throne in thy heart's deepest chamber.

LXXXIV

Thou art in space — someone must be,
Else thou wouldst not exist. Thy spirit
Abides in the Void that is all — in God.
And thou wouldst be nothing,
If, through God, multiplicity did not exist.
So behold, He manifests Himself, for otherwise the Good
Would remain hidden in Its unknown Selfhood.

The Good wishes to communicate Itself, for one should
On earth hear something of Heaven —
And may God turn His Grace towards the earth.

LXXXV

Agnostics brazenly maintain that we must
Believe that the intellect does not have the capacity to know.
A contradiction bordering on madness —
For whoever possesses intellect can know all.
Knowledge means: consciousness of this world
And of him who is conscious — because the Lord
Placed him in this selfsame world.

LXXXVI

Between God and the "I" is the Prophet.
Man as God, and God as Man, if one may put it thus.
The "I" means: Lord, forgive me;
Be grateful when evil turns away from thee.

The one who is conscious of his fault is dear to the Most High —
For humility, the Lord makes easy what is difficult.

LXXXVII

The Supreme Name is a ray of joy
That eases for thee the caprices of life,
And brings consolation midst the pain of all care.
Say: God — while sitting, lying or walking,
So says the Koran; whatever thou doest,
Wherever thou mayest be — thy heart will be born again.

LXXXVIII

Truth is man's great consolation;
In its wake, all beauty comes,
The noble splendor of high art —
For us, earth's children, many paths
Can lead to deep remembrance of God.

LXXXIX

Life is a Path from God to God —
Otherwise it is nothing. What more can I say?
And if life's burden weighs heavily on thee —
The All-Merciful will help thee to carry it.

Each day should be a Path from God to God —
Happy the man who can see himself thus.

XC

Love of the beautiful is not just blind emotion —
See to it that it be something better for thee.
What counts is not only that one should see the beautiful —
But also that one should reject the ugly,
Both outwardly and inwardly. For this must be clear:
Worthwhile is not what pleases everyone —
But only what, deeply inwardly, is good and true;
God made the good in the world from Truth.

XCI

Māyā and *vairāgya* — the Sanskrit words
For illusion and dispassion. The first is the world,
The second is the wise man's soul,
Which Brahma placed into illusion —
So that, in spite of *Māyā*, it might be real;
So that it might choose its true identity.

XCII

The *Stella Matutina* stands in the sky
And, with its brilliance, seeks to show us the way —
Not only to reach the desired shore,
But also to ascend to the kingdom of Heaven.

Forget not what the symbol means —
It guides the soul to the True Star.

XCIII

The traveler no longer knew where he was;
It was a joyless place —
Ma per trattar del ben ch'i' vi trovai,
Dirò de l'altre cose ch'i' v'ho scorte.

This means: one can find good in everything.
Certainly, life is not child's play;
One may often think that things go too far —

May our wayfaring unite us with God.

XCIV

The eye is not made for looking at God —
Whoever looks at the sun for long becomes blind;
Thou see'st God only with the eye of the heart.
The outward eye can see only visible things.

XCV

In the sky shines the sun which God conceived
As the image of another Sun, whose light
No earthly eye can reach —
Earth cannot see Divine Mystery.

The sun's splendor, standing proudly in the sky,
Is not eternal — see how it sets.

XCVI

Almost terrifying is the sky
That thou see'st at night in the Far North —
When, in the limitless, the spirit's eye
Reads the myth of the whole creation.

XCVII

When one is young, it is difficult to imagine
How an old person feels. And the old person should know:
He is standing with both feet on holy ground;
And may God forgive his despondency.
He must not be saddened by the weakness of age —
His trust in God must be an example.

XCVIII

"Beauty is the splendor of the True" —
And Truth is the essence of the beautiful:
This conclusion is implicit in Plato's thinking.
He did not wish to spoil us —
He wished to give us the doctrine in one phrase.

XCIX

Humility is the cord that holds together
All the beads — the other virtues;
So said the Curé d'Ars. If the cord breaks —
See how the array of virtues collapses into nothing.

C

Someone said to the Maharshi:[3] thou art full of illusion —
Thou art no master. The Maharshi laughed and said:
If there were no false masters in the world,
False disciples would not have their teachers.

CI

Thou must not be possessed by thine ego —
So think of the One Reality,
And remember that, in essence, thou art not
Other than this One — not other than beatitude.

CII

The wisest of men is liberated,
But he too has an ego.
Equilibrium is human nature —
Noble I-consciousness transcends itself.

CIII

Truth, and activity in accordance with it — the equilibrium
That holds together all that thou art;
If once thou hast known the True,
Thank God, and do what pleases Him.

CIV

Certitude and peace — these are the concepts
Which, on the basis of truth, contain our happiness,
And indeed everything. As for the world of doubters —
Let it be their world.

CV

Man, woman. Man is a creator —
He is the creator of the greatest human works.
Woman feels her vocation in other things:
Her happiness is to bring happiness to others.

CVI

Humility and goodness are offered by Nature —
God grant that such a man may also be strong
In what he does, for weakness leads to nothing.
Pride and wickedness are from the devil.

CVII

One of the most contemptible things
Is pettiness regarding vanquished enemies.
A noble conqueror, like Saladin,
Makes vanquished foes his friends —
For nobility brings benefits to both sides.
And if it is a devil that one has vanquished,
The punishment can yet bear noble features;
For what the revenge-thirsty man forgets is that
He who is noble, shows moderation in all.
Thou canst not be truly victorious in war,
If thou know'st not how to conquer thyself.

CVIII

I would prefer not to speak of bad things —
But they are there, and I must take account of them.
So let us talk of things that are useful —
But one cannot teach without saying "no."

CIX

Thou art woven into a particular time,
And must experience what others dream;
Then suddenly, after all the up-and-down and to-and-fro,
The nightmare vanishes —
No golden apples hung on the trees.
What once was real — it is no more.

CX

The world is a hierarchy of spheres —
The higher penetrates the one that follows it;
Creation goes from above to below,
And not from left to right on the same plane.

Gnosis teaches the emanation of light;
The spheres of the universe are contained in us.
But modern science knows nothing
Of God's Hands which fashion the universe —

Of all the wonders of the Divine Power.

CXI

Above all: hold fast to the Absolute;
For the contingent follows in its wake.
Were thy life but a single instant —
God would ask of thee the Absolute alone.

CXII

Discouragement is human, but one should remember,
That everything can lead the heart to the Good.
Even if thou art afraid of the world and of life —
Thou canst always find joy within the Creator.

CXIII

Do not think that the good of Knowledge
Will rob thee of everything else in life —
That God, when He has given thee the Truth,
Will not also give thee the good of Beauty.

CXIV

Human beauty is given by God;
One must live it in keeping with the Lord's intention —
Noblesse oblige. That the outward is good
Only has meaning if the heart reposes in the Most High.

Sometimes the evil one takes on a beautiful form,
So that the soul imagines that it is normal and perfect.
But perfection is not cheap —
The path to perfection is long.

CXV

Thou would'st like the world wheel to be better,
In things both great and small;
In vain — for it turns as destiny wills;
The wheel of existence cannot do more than this.

Be that as it may — make thine own soul pure;
Then, even if thou be small, something
On this poor earth will be better.

CXVI

There are women who are afraid of men,
Not knowing that there are two kinds:
The man who wants to enjoy women —
Then the man who loves the eternal feminine,

Without merely seeking possession or pleasure,
And who, in everything, is conscious of the Divine Essence.

CXVII

Knowledge and certitude are inborn in thee,
But nearby was always a shadow that hates the True,
As is the nature of things. But be of good cheer —
God will make thy burden lighter;
For whoever loves the True, is chosen.

CXVIII

A Master, over a hundred years old —
A saint in the land of the Siamese —
Has, through friends, sent me his greeting;
He has never been in my proximity.
It makes me happy to praise this wise man,
Even though I live far from his land.
For the striving of both of us is to the Above;
Brethren in Wisdom ever clasp hands.

CXIX

Spring is approaching and the birds greet it
                    High in the trees;
Thou see'st and hearest: the robin's joyous song
                    Would not miss it.
There is no need to ponder
                    The wish of thy heart;
Eternal spring, created by the Lord,
                    Thou carriest within.

CXX

Truth demands virtue;
Likewise, love follows from beauty.
All this is present in wisdom and nobility.
In the treasury of the heart lies Paradise.
And even if this heavenly kingdom seems too small for thee —
Then let the Lord enter in thy stead.

CXXI

If thou art happy in this life, dost thou know
How thou wilt experience its last word?
But God is always there. If thou knowest this,
Deo gratias — be happy with thy lot;
For God is That which is. Whether thou art here or not —
The Hand of the Most High will provide.

CXXII

One person loves philosophy, and at the same time
Scorns music — but something is missing here;
Another knows that music contains
What speaks to anyone who strives toward Heaven —
It is wrong to fragment the nature of things.

CXXIII

Beyond good and evil is All-Possibility —
Therefore whatever is, is in essence good,
For it cannot but be; and what must be,
Is like a play of Infinity.

CXXIV

A curious saying in the "Lord's Song":
"I am the guile of the deceiver";
How can the *Bhagavad-Gītā* say
That God is in the act of the liar?

Even the most stubborn deceiver would be
Incapable of lying, were there not in him
A spark of Divine Power; man can do nothing of himself,
Even when he acts outside honor.

CXXV

The stupidly proud man is always ready
To consider himself the salt of the earth;
He will split hairs over his glory —
Nothing is more despicable than vanity.

CXXVI

Whatever you admire in the outward world
Is prefigured, in a perfect way,
In the Lord. And is also reflected within yourselves;
Thus hope that God will show you even greater favor —

That our soul, O Lord, be like Thy Kingdom.

CXXVII

"To give is more blessed than to receive."
What do these words of Scripture tell us?
That in magnanimity — and man is free —
The giver surpasses himself.

CXXVIII

The greatest ones, those who are unforgettable,
Are the ones who give. But the good man,
Who faithfully accomplishes what for him is a duty and a path,
Is also a giver — he is so in the way that he can.

CXXIX

Do not think that what I say here of myself
Lacks modesty or is exaggerated:
All that one finds in good old books
Regarding Being, and the question of the universe,
God has inscribed in the substance of my heart.

CXXX

I have for long wished to end this book —
I could not do so; I had to write more poems.
But this time my pen lies down of itself,
For there are other preoccupations, other duties;
Be that as it may, whatever we may wish to do:
Let us follow the call of the Most High —

Let us repose in God's deep Peace.

Notes

Notes to *World Wheel IV*

1. Each language is a "soul," according to Aristotle.

Notes to *World Wheel VI*

1. In German: *Verstand, Vernunft, und reiner Geist.* The German word *Geist* means Spirit or Intellect; here, the *intellectus purus*.

Notes to *World Wheel VII*

1. Hungarian: traditional dance.
2. Arabic: member of the 'Isāwī spiritual brotherhood.
3. Shrī Rāmana Maharshi (1879-1950), Hindu sage.

Editor's Note: A few poems do not appear in this edition, but the original order and numbering have been retained.

Index of Foreign Quotations

Adonai Elohenu, Adonai Ehat (Hebrew): "The Lord our God, the Lord is One" (p.145).

Allāh karīm (Arabic): "God is generous" (p.123).

Alt Heidelberg, du Feine (German): "Old Heidelberg (old city in South Germany), you beautiful one" (p.109).

Beauté oblige (French): "Beauty obliges" (p.35).

Béni soit son saint Nom (French): "Blessèd be His Holy Name" (p.59).

Brahma Satyam (Sanskrit): "God is real" (pp.109, 113).

Brahma Satyam; jagan mithyā (Sanskrit): "God is real, the world is appearance" (pp.134, 145).

Cuando Dios quiere (Spanish): "When God wills" (p.29).

Deo gratias (Latin): "Thanks be to God" (pp.113, 165).

Errare humanum est; perseverare diabolicum (Latin): "To err is human, but to persevere in error is diabolic" (Seneca the younger); *Humanum fuit errare, diabolicum est per animositatem in errore manere*: "To err was human but to remain in error because of passion is diabolic" (St. Augustine, Sermon 164, 14) (p.47).

Frihet gar ut fron den ljungande Pol (Norwegian): "Freedom comes from the thunderous pole" (p.58).

Hamīn ast (Persian): "It is here" (p.58).

Il nome del bel Fior ch'io sempre invoco (Italian): "The name of the fair flower that I always invoke." From Dante's *Divina Commedia, Paradiso XXIII*.88 (p.85).

Insignifiant est ce qu'on exagère (French): "What one exaggerates loses its meaning" (p.29).

Lā ilāha illā 'Llāh (Arabic): "There is no divinity but God" (p.145).

Le coeur qui tend vers Dieu, n'a rien à craindre (French): "The heart which turns to God has nothing to fear" (p.19).

Le français définit; l'allemand veut peindre / Dans l'Esprit les génies devraient se joindre (French): "French defines, German seeks to paint, the geniuses [of the two languagues] combine in the Spirit" (p.19).

Ma già volgeva il mio disio e'l velle / Sì come rota ch'igualmente è mossa / L'amor che muove il sole e l'altre stelle (Italian): "But now my desire and will were turned / like a wheel that is evenly moved, / by the Love that moves the sun and the other stars." From Dante's *Divina Commedia, Paradiso XXIII*.143-145 (pp.35, 146).

Ma per trattar del ben ch'io vi trovai, / Dirò de l'altre cose ch'io v'ho scorte (Italian): "But in order to treat of the good that I found there, / I will speak of other things that I saw." From Dante's *Divina*

Commedia, Inferno I.8-9 (p.158).

Nel mezzo del cammin di nostra vita / Mi ritrovai per una selva oscura (Italian): "Midway along the journey of our life / I woke to find myself in a dark wood." From Dante's *Divina Commedia, Inferno* I.1-2 (pp.35, 138).

Noblesse oblige (French): "Nobility obliges" (p.163).

Nūr 'alā nūr (Arabic): "Light upon light." Koran 24:35 (p.118).

Om namo sarva Tathāgata Om (Sanskrit): "Hail to those who are 'thus gone,' hail" (p.99).

Om, Shānti, Om (Sanskrit): "Hail, Peace, hail" (p.42).

Ora et labora (Latin): "Pray and work" (p.114).

Per animositatem (Latin): "Because of passion"; *see also* "*Errare est humanum*" (p.47).

Requiescat in Pace (Latin): "May he rest in peace" (p.104).

Stella Maris (Latin): "Star of the sea" (p.107).

Stella Matutina (Latin): "The morning star" (pp.108, 157).

Vacare Deo (Latin): "To be empty in God" (pp.53, 147).

Vincit omnia Veritas (Latin): "Truth conquers all" (p.113).

Yā Latīf (Arabic): "O Most Gentle Subtle Lord" (p.124).

Yatra Krishna, tatra dharma, jaya (Sanskrit): "Where Krishna is, there is the victory of virtue" (p.79).

Index of First Lines

Poetry by Frithjof Schuon

Sulamith, Berna, Urs Graf Verlag, 1946
Tage- und Nächtebuch, Berna, Urs Graf Verlag, 1946
The Garland, Abodes, 1994
Road to the Heart: Poems, World Wisdom Books, 1995
Liebe, Verlag Herder Freiburg im Breisgau, 1997
Leben, Verlag Herder Freiburg im Breisgau, 1997
Glück, Verlag Herder Freiburg im Breisgau, 1997
Sinn, Verlag Herder Freiburg im Breisgau, 1997
Amor y Vida. Poesías, Mallorca, José J. de Olañeta, Editor, 1999
Sinngedigchte/Poésies didactiques, Volumes 1-10,
Sottens, Suisse, Editions Les Sept Flèches, 2000-2005
Songs for a Spiritual Traveler: Selected Poems, World Wisdom, 2001
Adastra & Stella Maris: Poems by Frithjof Schuon, World Wisdom, 2003
Autumn Leaves & The Ring: Poems by Frithjof Schuon, World Wisdom, 2007
Songs without Names: Volumes I-VI, World Wisdom, 2006
Songs without Names: Volumes VII-XII, World Wisdom, 2006
World Wheel: Volumes I-III, World Wisdom, 2006
World Wheel: Volumes IV-VII, World Wisdom, 2006

Books by Frithjof Schuon

The Transcendent Unity of Religions
Spiritual Perspectives and Human Facts
Gnosis: Divine Wisdom
Language of the Self
Stations of Wisdom
Understanding Islam
Light on the Ancient Worlds
In the Tracks of Buddhism
Treasures of Buddhism
Logic and Transcendence
Esoterism as Principle and as Way
Castes and Races
Sufism: Veil and Quintessence
From the Divine to the Human
Christianity/Islam: Essays on Esoteric Ecumenicism
Survey of Metaphysics and Esoterism
In the Face of the Absolute
The Feathered Sun: Plains Indians in Art and Philosophy
To Have a Center
Roots of the Human Condition
Images of Primordial and Mystic Beauty: Paintings by Frithjof Schuon
Echoes of Perennial Wisdom
The Play of Masks
The Transfiguration of Man
The Eye of the Heart
Form and Substance in the Religions

Edited Writings of Frithjof Schuon

The Essential Writings of Frithjof Schuon, ed. Seyyed Hossein Nasr
The Fullness of God: Frithjof Schuon on Christianity,
ed. James S. Cutsinger
Prayer Fashions Man: Frithjof Schuon on the Spiritual Life,
ed. James S. Cutsinger
Art from the Sacred to the Profane: East and West
ed. Catherine Schuon